# OTTO MICHAEL KNAB'S FOX-FABLES

Bernard M. Knab

Illustrations by James Brunsman

New Introduction by Ulrich Lehner

WIPF *&* STOCK · Eugene, Oregon

Wipf and Stock Publishers
199 W 8th Ave, Suite 3
Eugene, OR 97401

Otto Michael Knab's Fox-Fables
By Knab, Bernard M.
Copyright©1966 by Knab, Bernard M.
ISBN 13: 978-1-5326-3293-8

Publication date 8/24/2017
Previously published by Washington State University Press, 1966

# LIBRARY OF FORBIDDEN BOOKS—VOLUME 2

**The Library of Forbidden Books** publishes texts that totalitarian regimes have censored, prohibited, or labeled as dangerous.

Historical introductions contextualize these reprints or first-time translations, making this series suitable for advanced undergraduate and graduate classes, where a discussion of primary sources is desired.

# ACKNOWLEDGEMENTS

I am indebted to Otto Michael Knab for his assistance and continuous cooperation during the preparation of this book. He spent many hours providing me with biographical information and explaining the circumstances surrounding the writing of the *Fuchsenfabeln*, and assisted immeasurably during my labors through the first draft of the translation.

I am most grateful to John Elwood, Arne Lindberg, and Henry Grosshans for their valuable assistance and criticism during the preparation of the manuscript, and to Gertrud Mazur and Milton Petersen for their generous assistance in a number of problems. My wife Sharri has been much more than an able typist; many of her suggestions have been incorporated into the translation.

To James Brunsman I owe a very special thanks. His perceptive and original illustrations were made on his own time, of which there is very little to spare.

Bernard M. Knab

July, 1966

Pullman, Washington

Contents

# INTRODUCTION

## THE FORGOTTEN DIMENSION OF CATHOLIC EXILE LITERATURE

*The Case of Otto Michael Knab (1905–1990)*

BY ULRICH L. LEHNER

IF ONE PROBES INTO a history of German literature one will look for the name of Otto Knab in vain; likewise, if one searches for him in most works on the history of Nazism. Yet, in 1933-34 he had caused a stir with his satire *Kleinstadt unterm Hakenkreuz,* in which he recounts how the lovely village of Starnberg fell for the insanity of Nazism. He had fled to Switzerland, where he befriended Waldemar Gurian, a student of Scheler and arguably one of the most outspoken Catholic critics of the Hitler regime. Together the two exiled Catholics edited the *Deutsche Briefe,*[1] the most important Catholic exile journal, informing the world in a variety of languages about the cruelties of the regime between 1934 and 1938. Neither editor shied away from calling out German bishops for collaborating with the regime. After Gurian left for the United States in 1937 to take up a professorship at the University of Notre Dame, Knab was for a short while the sole editor until the increasingly volatile political atmosphere in Switzerland forced him to abandon this position.

1. Archive material on O. M. Knab can be found in his papers in the Archiv der Kommission für Zeitgeschichte, Bonn/Germany. On Knab's planned arrest by the Nazi police see Elke Fröhlich, "Redakteur am Starnberger 'Seeboten,'" in Elke Fröhlich and Martin Broszat (eds.), *Bayern in der Ns-Zeit,* vol. 6 (Munich and Vienna: 1983), 115–137. Other archive material is contained in the papers of Waldemar Gurian in the Library of Congress, Washington, DC; the papers of former chancellor Heinrich Brüning at Harvard University; the papers of Regina Ullmann in the Literaturarchiv Monacenisa, Munich; Deutsches Exilarchiv Frankfurt: American Guild for German Cultural Freedom. Material on the Committee for Catholic Refugees from Germany can be found in the H. Reinhold papers at Boston College, the Gordon Zahn papers at the University of Notre Dame, and the Center for Migration Studies/New York. The only edition of the *Deutsche Briefe* is Heinz Hürten (ed.), *Deutsche Briefe. Ein Blatt der katholischen Emigration.* 2 vols. (Mainz: Matthias-Grünewald-Verlag, 1969).

Knab also published three insightful novels, which the German literary critic Carl Muth put on par with those of Jeremias Gotthelf and Gottfried Keller.[2] Swiss author Hermann Hesse, Nobel Prize laureate for literature, even compared Knab's book *Ärgernis* (*Scandal*) in quality with George Bernanos' *Diary of a Country Priest*![3] Knab published first his twenty-one fables in the *Deutsche Briefe*, and they soon reached the status of classics. Here was a man who did not shy away from portraying Hitler as a shrewd fox, von Papen as vain ostrich, and Goebbels as parrot; of course, he did not do this to distract from their monstrous deeds, but rather to expose them to the ridicule they deserved and unmask their true, inhuman intentions. As a result, Knab lost his German citizenship and the possession of the *Deutsche Briefe* was criminalized as treason. Once Knab left for the United States in 1939, he soon stopped working for the exile opposition, simply because he needed to make a living and attend to other business. Neither the connections his friend Gurian provided nor the recommendations of Noble prize winner Thomas Mann and former German chancellor Josef Wirth were enough to establish him as an exile writer in the U.S. Also, the Committee for Catholic Refugees from Germany, which originally wanted to get Hollywood interested in making a movie out of Knab's novel *So einfach ist es nicht*, could not help, and seems to have ultimately dropped its support for him. Beate Viëtor even appealed to former chancellor German Heinrich Brüning, then already in his Harvard exile, to help, but to no avail.[4]

When Knab proofed the translation of the *Fox Fables* done by his son Bernard in 1966, he probably did not imagine that 50 years later, more than 25 years after his death, a reprint would make these again accessible. The series in which this reprint occurs is dedicated to reissuing books the Nazis

2. Center for Migration Studies, New York: CMS Collection #023B, Letter of Joseph D. Ostermann on behalf of the Committee for Catholic Refugees from Germany, 25 August 1939. See also the review by Adolf Fleckenstein, "Überwindung der Tragik. Zu einem vielgelesenen Roman," *Hochland* 35/1 (1937/38): 478–482.

3. Hermann Hesse, Letter to Otto Michael Knab of 26 February 1937, in Hermann Hesse, *Ausgewählte Briefe. Erweiterte Ausgabe* (Frankfurt: Suhrkamp, 1976), 169–170. See also the review essay by Leutfrid Signer, "Otto Michael," *Schweizerische Rundschau* 37 (1938): 201–204.

4. Paul Hoser, "Otto Michael Knabs Leben und sein Kampf gegen den Nationalsozialismus," in *Starnberger Hefte* Nr. 15 (2017): 15–55, at 46–47. Knab and Guarian had implored Brüning in the *Deutsche Briefe* to publish his memoirs to refute the Nazi propaganda about Hitler's rise to power. When the memoirs were finally published after Brüning's death in 1970, historians were largely disappointed by the distorted picture they presented.

deemed dangerous and consequently censored. Bernard Knab's excellent introduction and commentary, which give a concise overview of the work of his father, are included in this book. We thank Washington State University Press for permission to reprint of this long out-of-print publication.

It remains for me here only to point to the relevance of this book and to some recent research about Knab. Until today, Catholic writers in opposition to Hitler have not received much attention by scholars; only the most famous ones, like Reinhold Schneider, were acknowledged. The fact that Catholic writers like Gurian and Knab organized a network of kindred spirits, disseminated their message widely through Europe and the U.S., smuggled information and cooperated with active resistance fighters, was either forgotten or marginalized. Likewise, the fact that strongly Christian exile publishing houses existed, like the Lucerne *Vita Nova Verlag*, had been overlooked. Yet, one wonders if such opposition on the basis of Christian or Catholic principles looked different than the opposition of others; one wonders what exactly motivated these men and women and how they saw the future of Germany after Hitler. Only a thorough historical analysis could answer these and other questions, and also give us a fuller picture of the landscape of literary opposition, from which Catholic literature (and theology) seem to be glaringly absent.

Apart from this historiographical interest, the *Fox Fables* are a timeless masterpiece of political satire. They are a wake-up call to the fact that every democracy is fragile, and that one should never underestimate the shrewdness of those lusting for power and influence. For Otto Michael Knab, Nazism was not one political option among others, but a vicious assault on the Judeo-Christian worldview and any metaphysically grounded morality. It was a reversion to atavism, which also elucidates his choice of framing his critique in the form of animal fables.

Hopefully, this reprint will reignite also interest in the novels of Otto Michael Knab, whom contemporaries judged to be among the best of their time.

Otto Michael Knab

# CHAPTER ONE

# OTTO MICHAEL KNAB

On July 15, 1934, at five o'clock in the morning, Otto Michael Knab, editor-in-chief of the Starnberg *Land und Seebote,* escaped from his native Germany and crossed Lake Constance into Switzerland. A few days earlier, in the headquarters of Franz Buchner, the Nazi-appointed mayor of Starnberg, Knab had been presented an ultimatum. He was to publish and sign with his initials only articles and editorials that were either written or censored by Buchner's office—or be "finished" as editor of the *Land und Seebote.* Knab knew that "finished" almost certainly meant the concentration camp at Dachau. He knew also that he could not compromise his principles by agreeing to Buchner's terms. In order to gain time, he told Buchner he would comply with his demands. But then and there he decided to emigrate.[1]

Less than two years later, a series of beast fables began to appear in the *Deutsche Briefe,* a Swiss weekly press service edited by Waldemar Gurian and Knab. The man who for ten years had observed, as journalist, the machinations of Nazi politics was now writing, as fabulist, a satiric exposé of the Third Reich's rise to power. Knab called his extended beast narrative *Fuchsenfabeln (Fox-Fables).*[2]

Otto Michael Knab was born in Simbach am Inn, Germany, on March 16, 1905. His earliest years were spent in Munich with his adoptive parents, but soon after the death of his foster father, he was placed in an orphanage in Altötting. When he was about ten years old, Knab, in accordance with his foster mother's wishes that he become a priest, entered the Capuchin seminary at Burghausen. He lived in the seminary but attended classes at the German Royal State Gymnasium. Later he transferred to St. Stephan's Gymnasium in Augsburg. When he was fifteen, a clash with authority brought an end to his training for the priesthood. He was expelled from the seminary, and, as a result, his foster mother forbade him to go on with his schooling. He had to beg her for permission to finish the school year, and this he was finally allowed to do in the town of Landshut. After completion of this year, he was given the choice by his foster mother of becoming a shoemaker, a gardener, or a printer. "I chose printer because it was the closest to words. Subconsciously I knew that I wanted to work with words, though at the time I had, of course, no detailed plans for my life."[3]

Knab now began a four-year apprenticeship in the rural Bavarian town of Riedenburg. Although he was being trained in printing, he also took on journalistic assignments for the town's small newspaper. In 1924 he passed the required state examination for printers. When a relative informed him of an opening on a newspaper in Starnberg, Knab applied for the job, was hired, and began his ten years as "legman," assistant editor, and, eventually, editor-in-chief of the Starnberg *Land und Seebote*.

It was in these ten years (1924-1934) that Knab acquired many of the insights into contemporary events that he later utilized in writing the *Fuchsenfabeln*. He read widely and attended many public lectures. And as a journalist who had access to information not readily available to all citizens, he became more sharply aware of the true nature of Nazism. Knab was a Roman Catholic who, by 1929, had become editor-in-chief of a Catholic newspaper. What he consequently observed with special diligence was the German Catholic hierarchy's attitude toward the rising Nazi Party.

In the pre-Nazi period, the Church had officially forbidden Catholics to join the Party. A Catholic who joined the Party as a leader could be refused the sacraments and Christian burial. But when the Nazis came to power in 1933, the Catholic German hierarchy changed its tune literally from one day to the next. And when I saw that scores of Catholic journalists were suddenly left alone, sent to concentration camps, and no cock crowed after them, my fighting spirit awoke. And I realized then that we had to resist not only the Nazi regime, but also those who buckled under.[4]

The story of Knab's experiences as editor of a newspaper under the Nazi regime is a long and necessarily complicated one. What is of specific importance to a study of the *Fuchsenfabeln* is that Knab was for a number of years a close observer of the establishment of the Nazi state and that he saw through journalist's eyes the dissolution and corruption of political, social, and religious institutions under Hitler.[5]

Soon after his escape to Switzerland in July, 1934, Knab made contact with a well-known Catholic priest and author, Dr. Otto Karrer, who aided numerous refugees. Karrer helped secure Knab's certification as a political refugee, which allowed him to remain legally in Switzerland. And it was in Karrer's Lucerne home that the newly emigrated editor met Waldemar Gurian. Having read two of Gurian's books,[6] Knab was familiar with the author's name. Gurian soon indicated to his new friend that he was interested in establishing a literary instrument to fight Nazism from Switzerland. He wanted especially to influence Rome and the Catholic German hierarchy in whatever way possible. The result of this meeting between these two men was the establishment of the *Deutsche Briefe*, the

first number of which is dated October 5, 1934. The paper was to continue through 178 issues, ending with the edition dated April 15, 1938.[7]
Waldemar Gurian was the guiding spirit of the *Deutsche Briefe*. Knab was co-editor and contributor, and, after the summer of 1937, when Gurian emigrated to the United States and Notre Dame University, Knab carried on the enterprise alone for another ten months. The paper, usually about eight pages long, was a mimeographed weekly that appeared under the name of the now-defunct publishing house Liga-Verlag. In deference to the political neutrality of the Swiss Government, none of the material published in the *Deutsche Briefe,* including the *Fuchsenfabeln,* was ever signed. The *Deutsche Briefe* also functioned as a news service to approximately two dozen subscribing newspapers,[8] and there was a small number of individual subscribers who paid two Swiss francs monthly. The paper was addressed mainly to German readers, and its primary and consistent purpose was to explain the sources of Nazism's strength and to identify the anti-Christian forces at work in the contemporary world.[9] The editors obtained their information from governmental and ecclesiastical sources within Germany, and from a perusal of numerous German newspapers, periodicals, and books.

In addition to his work on the *Deutsche Briefe,* Otto Knab's literary output between 1934 and 1939 was remarkable. In 1934 he published *Kleinstadt unterm Hakenkreuz,* a journalistic account of how Nazi power was installed and secured in Starnberg am See. The book is a collection of true episodes told by the journalist who witnessed them, and published under the author's full name.[10] *Kleinstadt unterm Hakenkreuz* undertakes at the local, on-the-scene, journalistic level what the *Fuchsenfabeln,* written two years later, undertake creatively at the national level.

In 1935 Knab wrote his first work of fiction, *Der Mann in Holz,* a collection of stories held together by their "hero," a baroque confessional.[11] Next came a book for boys, *So einfach ist es nicht,* subtitled "Eine Geschichte von Mut und Übermut," which was translated into Dutch. Then followed, in 1936, Knab's most ambitious novel, *Ärgernis.* A second edition was published in 1937, and the novel was translated into Slovenian. The author sent a copy of his book to the Swiss Nobel Prize-winning novelist Hermann Hesse. In a letter written in German dated February 22, 1937, Hesse wrote Knab at length concerning *Ärgernis.* He said in part:

> It is the human and the Christian element that I love in this book. The moral and religious foundation upon which your book rests and out of which it has been created is strong and sound . . . throughout the book one can truly feel its austerity and truth.[12]

Knab also sent a copy of his book to Thomas Mann as a Christmas gift. Mann responded with a letter dated December 27, 1936, warmly thanking the young writer for the gift. In the letter he complains of the lack of time for his own, private reading. He then adds: "Aber ich habe schon manches aus Ihrem Buch aufgenommen und habe allen Grund, mir davon gute dichterische und menschlich vertiefte Stunden der weiteren Lektüre zu versprechen."

Knab next wrote *Die Stunde des Barabbas,* which was published in 1938.[13] With the exception of *Kleinstadt unterm Hakenkreuz,* a nonfiction work, and, of course, the *Fuchsenfabeln,* this relatively short, but beautifully controlled, symbolic story was perhaps the most immediately relevant of all of Knab's fiction to the increasingly threatening times. *Die Stunde des Barabbas* operates on three levels: the biblical-historical, the contemporary-historical, and the personal-spiritual. Knab intended the book as a message of hope in a moment of hopelessness, and it was so received by the critics. The leading Swiss newspaper, *Die Ost-Schweiz,* in a review dated December 10, 1938, wrote of the book:

A work that is a rousing and a frightening allegory, for the decisions in our time too. It is only a small book, but written with such dynamism, such concentration, such power of language, and such unity of religious and artistic capacity!

The Berne, Switzerland, newspaper, *Der Bund,* in its November 8, 1938, issue referred to Knab as one "who stands in the front ranks of German Catholic literature today." In a review of *Die Stunde des Barabbas* appearing in the same issue, the paper commented:

A poetic work not only in an aesthetic sense but in that total meaning of poetic that is literature's summons—a poetic work that is above all endowed with the timeless courage of spiritual confrontation and its consequences—as inexorable as life itself is inexorable.

And in a letter to Knab dated November 27, 1939, Hermann Hesse referred to the book as "this deep and beautiful creation . . . ."

By the time *Die Stunde des Barabbas* was published, its young author was being invited to read from his writings in cities throughout most of Switzerland: Zürich, Lucerne, St. Gallen, Berne, Basel, Fribourg, Zug, and many smaller towns. But if the Swiss were beginning to respond to the new writer by inviting him to read his works, the Nazis demonstrated their awareness of the man and his works by promptly placing his books on their index of unwanted literature.[14] In 1936 he was stripped of his German citizenship. As a result of these restrictions on the marketing of his books in Germany, none of Knab's works are listed in the bibliographies, catalogs, or anthologies of the German (Reich) literature of this period. He is listed only in *Deutsches Katholisches Schrifttum Heute,* published in 1936 by Benziger in Zürich, Switzerland, and in the *Salzburger Almanach,* published in 1937 by Anton Pustet, Salzburg, Austria.

The majority of Otto Knab's writings deal with his overriding concern with the meaning of Christianity. In his journalistic writings, and in *Die Stunde des Barabbas* where it is stated dramatically, Knab expressed his belief that the tragedy of the day was the Christian's failure to reject the new religion of Nazism, to refute it unequivocally through a firm adherence to Christian principles. And it is the heritage of Christianity that provides the moral basis for his other writings or that, as in the case of the *Fuchsenfabeln,* gives shape to the writer's vision not only of the world he satirizes, but the one he by implication posits as alternative; a world, in short, in which faith in God must be more than a hollow proposition.

Knab also engaged in other literary activities during these years. He frequently wrote poetry, much of which was published in Swiss newspapers and periodicals. He also wrote a number of novellen. And somehow he found time to lecture on contemporary German literature to an evening class in Zürich.[15] After the *Deutsche Briefe* was discontinued in the spring of 1938, Knab attempted to continue its policies in a new paper *Eidgenössische Besinnung,* which was addressed primarily to Swiss readers. The paper, however, lacked sufficient financial backing and had to be abandoned after only two issues. By this time it was also becoming increasingly dangerous for a German emigree-editor in Switzerland to publish direct criticism of Nazism, and the Swiss Government, too, was understandably becoming less cordial to such activities.

Knab, whose occupation was, in short, anti-Nazi writer, now realized that the increasingly uncomfortable political climate in Switzerland might very well necessitate his leaving the country. The mounting seriousness of events within Nazi Germany presented a threat to his personal safety, as well as to the safety of his entire family. He consequently applied for a visa in the spring of 1938 and received it on November 1 of that year. In January, 1939, he and his family left Europe for the United States.

Knab soon managed the always painful transition from one language to another. Within six months of his arrival in America he was invited to speak to various interested groups in South Bend, Indiana. Later he lectured in Boston and in many cities throughout New England. In the early 1940's,[16] Knab moved to the Pacific Northwest. He is presently publications editor in the Management Office of the Bonneville Power Administration in Portland, Oregon. He has recently completed translating a number of books from the German, treating of the Church's ecumenical reforms. In 1964 the Kommission für Zeitgeschichte bei der Katholischen Akademie in Munich notified Knab of its intention to publish in book form the entire 178 issues of the *Deutsche Briefe.*[17] This volume is now being prepared for publication in late 1966. Knab's *Fuchsenfabeln* are, of course, to be included in this new edition.

Notes to Chapter One

1

[1] Much of the information in this chapter was acquired in an interview with Mr. Knab on December 20, 1965.

2

[2] In their original form the fables carried the title *Fuchsen-Fibel—Fuchsen-Fabel (Fox - Primer — Fox - Fable)*. Throughout this book the general title *Fuchsenfabeln* is used.

3

[3] Knab, *Interview.*

4

[4] Knab, *Interview.*

5

[5] On July 14, 1934, the day before his escape, Knab wrote "Ein Leitartikel, der nicht mehr gedruckt werden darf." In this article he detailed for his readers the events that led to his decision to emigrate rather than to continue as editor under conditions laid down by the Nazis. He typed the article with as many carbons as he could manage, then mailed copies to friends asking them to recopy and/or distribute them as best they could in public places such as phone booths, post offices, and the like. In the ninetieth anniversary issue of the *Land und Seebote*, published on July 22, 1965, the paper printed Knab's last editorial for the first time. My translation of the article is included as Appendix 1 because it explains in detail Knab's struggle to continue as editor as long as he felt he could in conscience do so with any possible effectiveness. It also demonstrates Knab's proximity to events that he was later to satirize in his *Fuchsenfabeln*.

6

[6] *Der Katholische Publizist* (Augsburg, Verlag Haas Grabherr, 1931) and *Der Bolschewismus, Einführung in Geschichte und Lehre* (Freiburg im Breisgau, Herder, 1931).

7

[7] Knab's *Fuchsenfabeln* were printed in *Deutsche Briefe* Nr. 89 (June 12, 1936) through Nr. 102 (September 4, 1936). A more detailed treatment of the circumstances surrounding the writing of the fables and their distribution appears in Chapter 2.

8

[8] A partial list of these subscribing newspapers appears in Chapter 2.

9

[9] Some of the specific information on the *Deutsche Briefe* has been obtained from an article by M. A. Fitzsimmons in *The Review of Politics* (Vol. 17, January, 1955). In his article, "Die Deutschen Briefe: Gurian and the German Crisis," Fitzsimmons quotes extensively from numerous issues of the *Deutsche Briefe*. In the above reference to the paper's purpose, Fitzsimmons paraphrases Gurian's and Knab's own statement of purpose, which they published in the December 28, 1934, issue of the *Deutsche Briefe*.

10

[10] Knab says that upon leaving Germany he had made a pledge to his friends to work as much as possible outside German borders for a free Germany. In this true account of the takeover of his town by the Nazis, he chose to write under his full name in order to stand behind the facts and make good his pledge to his friends. The book was immediately banned in Germany.

11

[11] This is the first of Knab's works to be written under his pen name, Otto Michael. After settling in Switzerland, Knab soon realized that a writer could not subsist if he wrote in German for an exclusively Swiss audience. Since the Nazis were already familiar with the name Otto Michael Knab, the author knew that he would need a new name if he were to have his books distributed in Germany. He consequently adopted the abbreviated version of his full name for a pen name. He used this name for his novels, poems, occasional essays, and novellen. For articles that required a signature but not a full name, he used O. M., although he reserved this principally for articles of a religious na-

ture. For political and other articles, he used the letter "p" ("p" = "puer" = "Knab[e]" = "boy").

12
[12] The translation from the Hesse letter is mine. This letter and the letter from Thomas Mann are in Knab's possession. He has given me permission to quote from them in this study.

13
[13] *Die Stunde des Barabbas* was also translated into Slovenian. In 1943, in collaboration with Alexander Scharbach, Knab prepared an English version, which was published in that year by Sheed and Ward and entitled *The Hour of Barabbas.*

14
[14] Knab's books were put in the third or fourth category of this index. The third category included literature produced by Germans not in agreement with Nazi philosophy (though not overtly anti-Nazi) and authors published outside of Germany whose identity was not known to the Nazi Government, i.e., pen-name writers. These books could be stocked and reviewed in Germany, but no advertising of any kind was permitted them. The fourth category of the Nazi index included all clearly anti-Nazi books, and these were unqualifiedly *verboten.* Knab's *Kleinstadt unterm Hakenkreuz* and *Die Stunde des Barabbas,* as well as all issues of the *Deutsche Briefe,* were in this fourth class.

15
[15] A synopsis of the course, listing Knab as lecturer, can be found in the winter-semester program (1938-1939) of the *Katholische Volkshochschulkurse, Zürich.*

16
[16] During the early years of the war, Knab was invited by Jacques Maritain to co-sign the *Manifesto on the War,* a document by European Catholics sojourning in America and Canada. The *Manifesto* was signed by a distinguished list of men and women, among them Yves Simon, Sigrid Undset,

Waldemar Gurian, Georges Theunis, Charles Boyer, Frank Sheed, and Dietrich Von Hildebrand. The *Commonweal* (Vol. XXXVI, No. 18, August 21, 1942) devoted the majority of this issue to a reprinting of the major portion of the text, including also an extensive list of its signers.

17
[17] The new edition of the *Deutsche Briefe* will be published in the Veröffentlichungen der Kommission für Zeitgeschichte bei der Katholischen Akademie in Bayern, published by Konrad Repgen, Reihe A, Quellen, Matthias Grühnewald-Verlag, Mainz.

# CHAPTER TWO

# COMMENTARY

# I

When Otto Knab began writing the *Fuchsenfabeln*, his familiarity with fables was in no way extraordinary. Although he had read fables as a child, and was familiar with Aesop, La Fontaine, and Goethe's *Reineke Fuchs*, he was conscious of no particular influence when he began to use the genre to expose some of the sinister aspects of the Third Reich's rise to power. He does recall that in the mid-thirties there was talk about some fables being written in Italy by an anonymous anti-fascist writer.[1] Knab never saw these fables, nor did he know who wrote them. But hearing that someone was using the fable as a political weapon under similar circumstances no doubt encouraged him to go ahead with his own ideas for the genre.

In choosing a genre that utilizes beasts who act like people who in turn act like beasts, Knab selected a form that has been used in many ways: as social satire, as fairy tale, and as political or religious satire. No one knows definitely whether Aesop's fables were written to emphasize political, social, religious, or simply moral points. We do know, however, that Goethe's *Reineke Fuchs* was intended as a satire on the people and leaders of the French Revolution. La Fontaine had his eye on the whole of seventeenth-century French society. And George Orwell published a beast allegory indicting Russian communism in particular, and totalitarianism in general. Otto Knab planned to show by means of his fables how the Third Reich began and secured its power base, and how the various levels of society reacted to the totalitarian thrust.

Knab had undoubtedly been thinking of using the fable as a political weapon for longer than he was fully aware when he began writing the *Fuchsenfabeln*. In recalling the circumstances surrounding their writing, he was genuinely surprised to find that he had in early 1934 written two beast fables for his paper.

Funny thing. I had forgotten all about these earlier fables until I discovered them again in going through my papers. I had written a "Peep" story similar to the one in the *Fuchsenfabeln,* and had also done a little story using a woodpecker. These, of course, were published in the *Land und Seebote* only, never in Switzerland. But they are linked with the *Fuchsenfabeln,* since they were probably instrumental in leading me to the fable form once again.[2]

Knab was moved to take up the fable once again mainly by external circumstances. As an emigrant of Hitler's Germany and as co-editor with Waldemar Gurian of a weekly paper devoted to an analysis of National Socialism, Knab was committed to making his readers aware of the real nature of Nazism. As journalist, however, he was also aware of one condition over which he had little control: the majority of the people simply would not take the time to read analytical, political editorials, no matter what their content., But the fables occurred to Knab as a possible means to exercise at least some control over what would and would not be read. He could see that those readers who could not be relied upon to read an analytical article might well succumb to the appeal of a story.

Knab had written a number of the fox fables as early as the fall of 1935. In a prefatory paragraph to the first fable, he wrote: "The *Fuchsenfabeln* were already written in 1935, but they become increasingly intelligible day by day. Today we begin printing the first in a series containing twenty fables."[3] This statement is slightly misleading if taken quite literally. What it does indicate is that Knab had a general scheme for the *Fuchsenfabeln* well worked out by the time he began printing them in the *Deutsche Briefe.* But one of the fables, *The Foolish Cousins,* deals with the Spanish Civil War, which did not begin until the summer of 1936, and therefore it could not have been written in 1935 as Knab's brief preface would indicate. And there are twenty-one fables, not twenty as the introduction states; *The Much-Traveled Bison* was added after Knab had written the introductory comments. These apparent contradictions are explained by the fact that the *Fuchsenfabeln* were not printed in book form, but were included as a part of the contents of the *Deutsche Briefe* throughout the summer of 1936. Knab recalls that he had written from six to ten fables and had a rough outline of the rest in mind when he wrote his prefatory comments introducing the printing of the first fable. However, the content of the later fables in particular, like the content of articles in the *Deutsche Briefe,* was often determined by constantly changing and worsening events in Germany. As the summer of 1936 wore on, events such as the Civil War in Spain led Knab to abandon certain originally planned fables and to replace them with fables he felt were more timely and relevant.

The editors of the *Deutsche Briefe* decided to smuggle copies of the *Fuchsenfabeln* into Germany separately in hope of achieving a wider circulation with them than could normally be expected from the analytical articles which comprised their press service.[4] By chopping off the mast-head reading *"Deutsche Briefe"* and leaving only a headline "Fuchsenfabeln," they enhanced their chances of retaining their anonymity as editors of a radical, Catholic weekly, and for eluding immediate Gestapo censorship once the fables were smuggled across the border.

While the journalist in Knab recognized in the fable a means by which to secure a large audience, the poet in him sensed the possibilities of the genre's built-in devices for creating a fictional world that would parallel the real world of Nazi totalitarianism. He could create a fox-demagogue who would speak in the style of Hitler and the Nazi propagandists. He could people his animal world with other characters who would represent the easily recognizable historical figures of the day. One story could build upon the next. Now these rational beasts could be made to demonstrate the stupidity, perversity, or blindness of their historical parallels. The ironies contained not only in the genre, but also in the given moment in history, would mix and compound themselves freely. The fables could entertain and evoke laughter—even cruel laughter—and the reader could respond to them by feeling a certain sense of moral superiority to the characters by seeing through them and their methods.

Knab, then, regarded the *Fuchsenfabeln* as a means to an end. Although a number of fables went through a first draft, some were written as an immediate response to new developments in Nazi Germany. Knab would sometimes work these out in his mind on the train trips between Walchwil, where he lived, and Lucerne, where the *Deutsche Briefe* were published, and then type them at the first opportunity directly onto the mimeograph stencil along with other articles being prepared for the *Deutsche Briefe*.

# II

Otto Knab's *Fuchsenfabeln* continue to be meaningful beyond the specific moment in history for which they were written. Knab wanted to expose many of the sinister features of the Third Reich's rise to power and society's reaction to these phenomena. He set out to create with the fables a fictional world that would in turn mirror the real world of Nazi totalitarianism. He succeeded in this attempt, but he also created a fictional world that is almost timeless. It is quite possible to examine the *Fuchsenfabeln* in detail, and to point here and there and say: "The fox is Hitler. The ostrich is von Papen. 'Six days after the summer solstice' refers to the Blood Purge of June 30, 1934." Yet after all this has been said, the fables remain as something still more: a fictionalized representation of man's willingness, not only to allow, but to subject himself to a totalitarian demagogue and the system he imposes. The mere removal of the im-

Auf das an die Deutsche Gesandtschaft
in Bern gerichtete Schreiben vom 31.v.M.

                    Herrn

                    Otto  K n a b ,

                    Ligaverlag

                    _ _ _ L u z e r n _ _ _ _

                    Postfach 391.

        Nach einer im Deutschen Reichsanzeiger und Preussischen
Staatsanzeiger Nr. 171 vom 25. v. M. veröffentlichten Bekannt-
machung des Reichs- und Preussischen Ministers des Innern vom
22. v. M. ist unter andern ein Herr Otto  K n a b , geboren
16. III.1905, auf Grund des § 2 des Gesetzes über den Wider-
ruf von Einbürgerungen und die Aberkennung der deutschen
Staatsangehörigkeit vom 14.VII.1933 der deutschen Reichsange-
hörigkeit als verlustig erklärt worden, weil er durch sein
Verhalten, das gegen die Pflicht zur Treue gegen Reich und
Volk verstösst, die deutschen Belange geschädigt hat.

        Sollten Sie mit dem Genannten identisch sein, bitte ich
um Rückgabe Ihres Reisepasses und Ihres Heimatscheins.

        Der Reichsanzeiger steht mir nicht zur Verfügung, ich
stelle Ihnen ergebenst anheim, die betreffende Nummer durch
den Buchhandel zu beziehen.

                    Der Deutsche Generalkonsul

                    Im Vertretung:

Reproduction of the letter by which the German Consulate in Switzerland notified
Otto Knab of his expatriation.

# FUCHSEN-FIBEL  -  FUCHSEN-FABEL                                    1

Die "Fuchsenfabeln" sind bereits 1935 geschrieben worden, aber sie werden von Tag zu Tag verständlicher. Wir beginnen heute mit dem Abdruck der ersten Fabel der Reihe, die zwanzig Fabeln umfasst.

## Der Fuchs und die Füchse

Es war einmal ein Fuchs. Der tat nicht wie andere Füchse tun, lernte nicht das Handwerk seines Geschlechts und wollte nicht wie seine Brüder leben. Er fühlte sich zu Höherem geboren. Da er jedoch kein Gehör in seinem heimatlichen Fuchsbau fand, entlief er ihm und kam zu Verwandten. Als er nun aber in die Jahre gekommen und sein Gefühl mit ihm gewachsen war, versammelte er die Füchse, die er kannte, um sich und redete zu ihnen: Meine Genossen! Wir sind von gleicher Art, von gleicher Farbe. Rot ist unser Fell und Fuchsenblut fließt in unseren Adern. Wir sind ein edles Geschlecht,nein das edelste sind wir. Denn in uns verbindet sich die Klugheit unserer Ahnen mit der Kraft unserer Glieder und der Gesundheit unserer Gebisse. Ja, in uns verbinden sich Geist und Kraft. Wir gelten als das Vorbild der Schlauheit. Wir sind bekannt als Meister der Zähigkeit. Wir sind Helden! Jeder Einzelne von uns ist Heros! Aber warum, meine Genossen, warum,meine Füchse, sind wir nicht, was wir doch sein müssten nach all unseren Tugenden und nach dem Plane der Schöpfung? Warum sind wir nicht die führende unter den Rassen der Erde? Weil jeder seine Klugheit, seine Kraft und Zähigkeit gebraucht, um seinen eigenen eigensüchtigen Nutzen zu erjagen! Weil jeder seine Tüchtigkeit für sich verbraucht und nichts mehr übrig bleibt für die Gesamtheit, unsere Gesamtheit der Füchse! Und nun denkt, meine Genossen: Wenn jeder Einzelne von Euch schon so klug, so schön, so stark, so edel, so herrlich ist - wie klug und schön, wie stark und edel, wie herrlich müssten wir erst sein, wenn wir unsere Tugenden alle zusammenwürfen zu einer einzigen Tugend: der Kraft und Größe unseres Geschlechts der Füchse! Und wißt Ihr, meine lieben Fuchsgenossen, was dazu not tut? Wir müssen eins sein! Wir müssen einen Willen haben, einen einzigen Willen, den Fuchsenwillen! Keiner darf seinen eigennützigen Willen behalten! Das wäre Verrat. Fort mit dem verwerflichen Intellekt gewisser Füchse,der schuld ist an der entehrenden, unwürdigen Stellung unseres Geschlechts! Kein Fuchs hat ein Recht auf persönliche Klugheit, auf persönliche Fähigkeit! Nur die Gemeinschaft der Füchse ist die Trägerin der füchsischen Art, der füchsischen Tugend, des füchsischen Heldengeistes! Fort mit dem verwerflichen Einzelwillen, der uns um die Früchte unserer Rasse gebracht hat! Ein einziger Wille muß uns alle beseelen. Dieser eine Wille ist die Summe des edelsten Könnens und Wollens aller unseres Geschlechts. In mir, meine Füchse, verkörpert sich der Wille jedes Einzelnen von Euch! In mir verkörpert sich die Kraft und die Tüchtigkeit unseres ganzen ahnenstolzen Geschlechts. Ich bin Euer Führer! Ich bin Eure Zukunft! Ich bin Ihr! Wer echtes Fuchsenblut in seinen Gliedern hat, der glaubt an mich. Wer aber nicht an mich glaubt, der hat damit bewiesen, daß er kein Fuchs ist -sonst würde er an mich glauben! - dass fremdes, verfälschtes, geschändetes Blut in ihm kreist und dass er sich also selbst ausstösst aus unserer Gemeinschaft. Wer aber an mich glaubt, der wird nicht irre an mir. Auch wenn ich nicht stets wie ein Fuchs handle, bin ich doch immer ein Fuchs! Ja, auch wenn ich in die Haut unserer Feinde steige, bleibe ich ein Fuchs,und nur um unsere Feinde zu vernichten, kleide ich mich in ihre Haut und spreche ihre Sprache. Das ist Fuchsenschläue, wie sie die Welt nicht sah! Das ist Fuchsentreue, dass auch die Treue ein Spiel meiner Schläue ist! Euch aber, meine Füchse, führe ich zu einer neuen Zeit. Man wird davon noch rühmen in den fernsten Tagen, denn ich führe Euch entgegen dem Jahrtausend, dem ewigen Jahrtausend der Füchse! -

Der Fuchs hatte geendet. Er stand da, aller Füchse aller Zeiten größter Fuchs. Blitzschnell überlegten die anderen Füchse sich: Was? Wer ihm nicht folgt, der soll kein Fuchs mehr sein? Ich bin ein Fuchs! - Ich auch! -Ich auch! - Ich auch! - Und so erhob sich ein gewaltiger Lärm und durch den Jubel seiner Füchse schritt  d e r  Fuchs.

+

2.Fabel: "Der Strauß, der Fuchs, und nocheinmal der Strauss" und 3.Fabel: "Rat und Tat im Federvolk" in nächster Nummer.

A page from the *Deutsche Briefe* containing the first of the *Fuchsenfabeln*.

mediate historical disguises does not leave the fables stripped, for they continue to wear the more universal truths in which they were originally attired.

At least a part of the reason for the continuing effectiveness of the *Fuchsenfabeln* today is that the fictional world created in them was fashioned after the Nazi state, which became the cardinal example of the worst elements of totalitarianism. A successful indictment of Nazi totalitarianism would almost inevitably be an indictment of totalitarianism wherever it might appear. But a successful indictment still depends upon the shape its creator gives to what he observes and envisions.

The shape that Knab gave to his observations on the world he saw collapsing around him was in turn determined by his vision of what he believed the world should be. For before one can commit himself to a work that sets out to depict allegorically the ethical dissolution of society under a totalitarian regime, he must have a vision of what is ethical, what is good, and what is right. Knab's vision was grounded in his conception of Christianity, in his belief in the dignity of the individual who under no circumstances must surrender body and soul to an ego-maniacal madman. He regarded Nazism as a general assault on the Christian philosophy of life; surrender to National Socialism would, he felt, "result in the complete decomposition of one's moral existence."[5] This view he expressed in the majority of his writings, and it is once again strongly implied in the *Fuchsenfabeln*. There it manifests itself negatively through the omniscient narrator's ironic point of view. It is even more discernible in the concluding prophetic fable, which posits the likelihood of one totalitarian's violent demise at the hands of another. But nowhere is the author's view of the world more apparent than in the "epilogue." There, as if in spite of man's inhumanity, Knab's vision manifests itself more as a deep faith in God than as any intellectual assertion of man's potential for good. From the profound desolation of the apocalyptic, poetically developed scene there emerges a faith and hope in the Creator and his creation.

# III

The *Fuchsenfabeln* must be regarded as a whole; they are a cumulative, closely connected, extended beast narrative. Their continuity is maintained in part by the fox's presence in all but two of the fables, and in one of the two exceptions, *The Wise Owls,* he is directly referred to. After his long speech in the first fable, his demagoguery is firmly established, and through the rest of the narrative he continues to demonstrate his capacity for deceit or brutality or cynicism, or for entertaining delusions of grandeur. He evidences these and other characteristics primarily by reacting to the various factions that either want to join him or that appear to him to threaten his position. But after his long tirade in the first fable, a sense of inevitability is evoked from what he has revealed about himself. Nothing the fox does later really surprises; he is, from the first, the demagogue.

The character of the fox, then, provides a continuity for the fables. But other devices, for example, the use of time, are also employed to hold the narrative together. The thirteenth fable begins: "It was six days after the summer solstice had been celebrated in the empire of Fox." In the fifteenth fable, the migratory birds are about to begin their travels because winter is approaching their land. Later in this fable the birds return again, since the sun has reappeared in their homeland. A number of fables begin with a direct reference to a preceding fable. The second one, for example, starts: "In his zoo, Sir Ostrich was attending a footrace of gentlemanly young ostriches when news of Fox's plan first reached him." The twelfth fable follows the fable about the wise owls and begins: "It happened, however, that the owls' unanimous adoption of the new fox learning . . . ," and the continuity is assured. Sometimes either the narrative voice or the animals themselves refer to characters or events that appear in previous fables. In the fable about the migratory birds, the narrative voice remarks: "And they flew high over the passes of the fox empire into other lands where the fishes had not yet been made the example for all the animal kingdom." The reference is to the ninth fable in which the fishes are rewarded for their dumbness. When the fox is conniving with the weasel in *The Weasel,* he says: "The cardinal—you know, the one who flew the coop across the mountains." He is referring to an incident in *The Cardinal and the Birdlover* in which the cardinal quite willingly joined forces with the new fox community. In *Schoolmaster Fly and the Cuckoo Parents* the fox instructs: "You will not, as the schoolmasters of old, teach with loud speeches. My parrots will do that." The reference is to an earlier fable in which the parrots swarm out into the land, spreading the gospel according to Fox.

The sense of inevitability that is evoked in the course of the first fable continues to give tone to the entire series of *Fuchsenfabeln.* The ostrich "high-steps it" over to the fox and offers his services. The offer is accepted, and the fox proceeds to use the ostrich only so long as he has a need for him. In the third fable the members of the old, established leadership classes gather together to voice their righteous indignation at the upstart fox. They hem, haw, and stew just long enough to arrive at a solid commitment to nothing. Sometimes the sense of inevitability is toned with a degree of poignancy, as in *The Feeding.* Here the cruelty imposed by the minor fox officials upon the starving birds implies a great deal more than the specific action itself; the fox's demagoguery is evidenced in its effect upon the helpless. In the ninth fable, *How the Fishes Were Rewarded,* the sense of inevitability becomes uncomfortably grim; the fox praises the fishes for "being quietly, wordlessly willing to be devoured." In contrast to the harsh "zeegs" of the fox's henchmen, the fishes acknowledge the fox's cynicism by giving "fresh evidence of their virtue. They tolerated even this, and remained dumb."

The style of the *Fuchsenfabeln* varies from compressed simplicity to verbose hyperbole. In both these extremes, the style is deliberately appropriate to the content. Once again, *The Feeding* and *How the Fishes Were Rewarded* provide examples. In both these fables, the language is compressed and direct. And through this stylistic compression, the poignancy and grim humor of the action are made the more effective. In *The Parrot Plague* simplicity and hyperbole combine. The dialogue between the fox and Jako the parrot is crisp and to the point. But then the narrative voice steps in to describe the ensuing propaganda campaign, and the prose takes off in hyperbolic flight.

Their sharp beaks overflowed with what they had to say and the words dripped from their tireless, flapping tongues, flooding all creation, flowing through fields, forests, valleys, mountains, cities, villages, even to the remotest hamlet, inundating men and beasts alike . . . .

Sometimes the style is directly responsible for the humor in the fables. In *The Conference of the Crows,* "They dined, they conferred, they disputed, they debated, they strolled, and they dined again" occurs with little variation three times in as few as seven lines. It is the narrative voice again, delighting in exaggerated repetition, mocking those elements in the land that gather around the conference table to deliberate on their next course of inaction.

Only once does the style of the *Fuchsenfabeln* shift radically from the extremes mentioned above or anywhere between them. In the "epilogue" the poetically described desolation of the scene compels the reader to see the "stone plateau from which all greenery had been stripped and strewn about in every direction by the biting morning wind"—to see "where before millions of living things had bustled about in the mossy thickness, the sun now burned even the last damp patches dry until nothing remained but denuded stone." The effect of this scene upon the reader is that he is immediately drawn into it almost to the extent that he forgets the brutal passage immediately preceding—the fox's sudden annihilation by the wolf. The complete shift in scene and mood seems to underline the emptiness of the fox's and the wolf's malicious triumphs; they are forgotten, and, as if in spite of them, what is celebrated is the determination that gives even the tiniest living matter the will to live. From the mighty fox to a few tiny shreds of living lichen—the contrast is all the more effective because it is the lichen and all they represent that remain with the reader.

But the *Fuchsenfabeln* are satiric fables, and their style reflects this repeatedly in the parody that goes on in much of the animals' dialogue. The parody is perhaps most evident in the fox's long tirade to his new-found followers in the first fable. His speech parodies not only Hitler's speeches, but the general tone, style, and content of much other Nazi oratory. When the fox exclaims, "I am you! He who has genuine fox-blood flowing in his veins will believe in me," his language parodies Hitler's similar messianic oratory, which in turn was a conscious parody and mockery of Christ's message to his apostles. Near the end of the fable, the fox's prediction of an "eternal millenium of foxes" is another obvious example of Hitler's apocalyptic prose. In *The Envy of the Woodpeckers,* when the fox proclaims, "Now you have realized that I am the supreme judge of all," the language very nearly duplicates Hitler's pronouncement in his famous Reichstag speech of July 13, 1934: *". . . in this hour I was responsible for the fate of the German people, and I thereby became the supreme justiciar of the German people."*[6] The last speech in *Reporter Stork's Second Interview,* in which the fox babbles on and on about race, superiority, honor, and the right of domination, parodies the style and content of Hitler's ponderous *Mein Kampf.*

But parody is not what the *Fuchsenfabeln* are; it is but a stylistic device employed in them. And it is a stylistic device that adds to the already considerable irony that distinguishes each of the fables. Parody, satire, irony—throughout the *Fuchsenfabeln* these three elements are inextricably present. Consider the layered irony in *The Wise Owls.* The owls speak, act, and think like men, but they proceed to apply their rational faculties in such a way that they are led to a total effacement of their individual dignity. For they unanimously succumb like robots to the new fox *Weltanschauung.* These two levels of irony are, however, inherent properties of the fable as a form. But in *The Wise Owls* the irony becomes even more layered. The owls are the scholars in this fictional world, yet not one of them raises a voice in opposition to the rantings of Bubu, the fox's agent. All, in fact, sell out to the new "fox-dictates," which Bubu announces. They do more; they wholeheartedly embrace the new fox-learning to such an extent that each of them uncovers a system of his own that proves conclusively that the fox's teachings "had never been anything else than the great prophecy which had now been fulfilled." There is even added irony in the fact that the owls, the traditional symbols of wisdom, are chosen in this fable to represent science and scholarship. Here, in the land of fiction, the owls cannot even live up to their image as owls! And when Bubu exclaims, "Thus, the night of liberation has also arrived for science and scholarship," the irony created by the complicated word play is shrouded in grim humor.

Such many-layered irony occurs in the majority of the individual fables that comprise the *Fuchsenfabeln,* and it is through these ironies that truth is revealed. The reader responds to the many levels of irony operative in this land of fiction by recognizing truths that emerge as parallels to the follies committed by men in the real world around him. Furthermore the genre, fable, contains yet another feature that in part facilitates this response. Inherent in the fable is a quality of distance. The chicanery of the fox is easily transferable to the chicanery of the man. But it remains the fox's chicanery, nevertheless. Yet this distance between the fox and the reader is double-edged. Since everything occurs in a fictional world, the reader is removed from the events. But this very removal allows him the freer exercise of his objectivity, and hence the greater opportunity to respond to the truths illuminated through the layered irony. While he is being entertained, the reader is also being stimulated to an awareness of the evil that is being satirized. Hence, although the fables' author directed his satire specifically toward the Nazi state and its hierarchy, it reaches beyond immediate history and endures as an ironic comment on the general qualities of totalitarianism.

One of the distinctive features of Knab's fables is the selection of animals. There is little wonder that the fox was chosen to be the anti-hero of the *Fuchsenfabeln*. In the literature of the fable he has been playing the "heavy" for a long time. Even the English language owes the fox a noun, an adjective, and an adverb. The fox, so be it, is a crafty, cunning, sly, deceitful, shifty operator. He makes a fine Adolf Hitler, a fine demagogue. The ostrich, nervous, long-necked, and with a propensity for burying its head in the sand, is an ideal choice for the aristocratic von Papen, who, when he had served his purpose in the Reich, was given a post as ambassador to Austria. Von Papen possessed a not uncommon human frailty: he wanted to stay alive. To do so, he knew he had to remain useful. The fact that two of his assistants were murdered in the June 30, 1934, Blood Purge did not dissuade him from accepting the Austrian post. But in the fictional land of the *Fuchsenfabeln*, the ostrich is also representative of just one of the demagogue's many victims; he is the rather self-important character who is quick to seize an opportunity in the new scheme of things, who imagines great things for himself in the new system, and who is used by the system until he one morning discovers that he has served his purpose in the upper echelon. He does not react to his discovery violently; he is more prone to go along, to bury his head quietly and unobtrusively in the sand.

In a few of the fables, Knab's choice of animals is very particular and exact. The ichneumon flies, noted for their habit of laying their eggs into the larvae of other insects, are used in the fable *Schoolmaster Fly and the Cuckoo Parents* to satirize what went on in the Reich's educational policies, particularly primary education. They demonstrate as well the extent to which the demagogue will go in order to realize his ends. And in this same fable, Knab has included the cuckoos, known for laying their eggs in the nests of other birds, to expose the demagogue's readiness to subvert those elements that continue covertly to resist him. The butcher-bird, who in the fable *"Fuchs, Du hast . . ."* becomes the head of the fox's secret police, is, of course, a shrike. The shrike possesses the peculiar characteristic of impaling its victims on the thorns of its nest. In *The Cardinal and the Birdlover* the cardinal represents Monsignor Kaas, who was leader of the predominantly Catholic Center Party. Kaas was among other things instrumental in forcing his party's unanimous vote for the Enabling Act, which gave the Nazi Party the semblance of legality it needed to establish its power in the entire Reich. But the meaning of *The Cardinal and the Birdlover* is not confined to the immediate moment in history for which it was written; under any totalitarian regime, various factions, whether religious, educational, or political, will eventually be corrupted into compliance with the party line. There will always be a cardinal bird, who, whether blindly, stupidly or knowingly, will step forward to do the negotiating.

Although, as has been asserted here, Knab's *Fuchsenfabeln* succeed both on the historically immediate as well as on the timeless, creative level, some exceptions or qualifications to this assertion must be pointed out. There is one group that was very powerful in the real Germany but is conspicuously absent from the *Fuchsenfabeln*. There is no fable dealing specifically with the military. In a fictional presentation that depicts the rise to power of a demagogue and that describes the various reactions to this event, the absence of a separate fable for the military detracts from the total effect. If the fables are taken only as a satire on the Nazi state, the absence of a fable dealing specifically with the military is perhaps even more conspicuous. At the time Knab wrote the *Fuchsenfabeln* in 1936, Hitler was testing his military hardware in Spain, and the increasing might of the German Army was no longer a secret. And, of course, one of the most aggravating problems for Adolf Hitler from beginning to end was his constant altercations with the Wehrmacht.

Knab knew these things well. Perhaps he knew them too well. For it was in large part his antipathy to the military that made him decide not to include treatment of it in the *Fuchsenfabeln*. "I have no separate fable dealing specifically with the military. I knew that it was one matter in which I could not possibly remain even remotely objective."[7] Knab did, however, succeed in maintaining his objectivity when he satirized, in a number of places throughout the fables, the Nazi Party's para-military organizations: the S.S. and the Gestapo. In *How Fox Encountered the Various Animals* the black dogs, chosen by Fox to become his personal body-guards, represent the S.S., and in *"Fuchs, Du hast . . . ,"* the butcherbird represents Heinrich Himmler who in April, 1934, was appointed head of the

Prussian Gestapo, and Chief of the Federal Police by statute of June 17, 1936.

One of the features of the *Fuchsenfabeln* that accounts for much of their continuing effectiveness as an extended fable narrative is that the characters created in them inhabit a world of fiction in which word and action are accommodated to that created world's milieu. But there are at least four instances in the fables in which the real world trespasses into the land of fiction. One of these instances might best be described as a political slip of the tongue, and the other three are matters of geography. In *The Much-Traveled Bison*, the bison finally breaks his silence near the end of the fable by saying: "Yes, I am also a Bolshevik."[8] Earlier in this same fable, there is a reference to the Russian Caucasus. In *The Migratory Birds Begin Their Travels* the aristocratic birds take up residence at "the fashionable spas of the Baltic and North Seas." In *Reporter Stork's Second Interview*, the stork "who wrote everything down" scribbles madly while the fox raves on about the "sable of Siberia . . . the jackal of Africa . . . the wolf of the Asian steppes . . . and the blue-pelted Arctic fox." To make too much of these departures from the fictional realm of the fables would be foolish. But since the rest of them adhere as well as they do to a fictional world, these occasional infractions are all the more conspicuous, and they mar, although slightly, the *Fuchsenfabeln's* organic unity.

At least two fables, *The Cardinal and the Birdlover* and *How Fox Encountered the Various Animals,* conclude in the present tense: "he warbles and warbles, up to this very day" and "And this Fox has done to this very day," respectively. The fables were, of course, written in 1936 as a fictional parallel to an existing totalitarian state. The effect of the present tense on the contemporary reader might well be one of two kinds; he may be distracted by it, and see it as an intrusion on what is, for the most part, the timeless quality of the fables, or he may react by recognizing a certain grim humor in the contemporary applicability of what he reads.

As an extended beast narrative depicting a fox-demagogue's ascension to power and the animal society's reaction to the inevitable consequences of that ascent, Knab's *Fuchsenfabeln,* in spite of occasional flaws, continue to be vital and relevant beyond the specific moment in history for which they were intended. The author's extensive journalistic experience in Germany and Switzerland provided him with the historical insights necessary to satirize effectively existing political, social, and religious conditions.[9] And through his beast narrative, Knab demonstrated his understanding of the psychology of the human animal. He had known the fox, the ostrich, the cardinal, and many others. His *Fuchsenfabeln* are meaningful today and should be so beyond today because the general phenomenon they describe continues to be with us. Numerous variations of totalitarianism exist in pockets of infection the world over: in China, in Russia, in Germany, in the

United States—the list would be a long one, and would need to include a parish in Louisiana as well as the largest island in the Caribbean. When, for example, Knab wrote *Schoolmaster Fly and the Cuckoo Parents,* he wrote a fable that applies in our own time just as surely as it applied to Hitler's Germany.

## Notes to Chapter Two

1

[1] This writer was very probably the Italian poet Carlo Alberto Salustri (1873-1951) who was writing beast fables in the thirties under the pen name Trilussa. It is significant that two poets, at almost the same time, chose the fable as the means to voice their critical and satirical response to the menace of dictatorial power.

2

[2] Knab, *Interview.* See Appendix 2 for my translation of these early fables.

3

[3] *Deutsche Briefe* Nr. 89 (June 12, 1936).

4

[4] The distribution of the *Fuchsenfabeln* was, however, not confined to the editors' personal efforts to smuggle them separately into Germany. The *Deutsche Briefe* had a number of European, Catholic newspapers as regular subscribers (for example, *Der Deutsche in Polen,* published in Kattowitz; *Der Deutsche Weg,* published weekly in Holland by the Jesuit Father Friedrich Muckermann; *Elsässischer Kurier,* Colmar, Alsace; and the *Linzer Volksblatt,* Linz, Austria). These and other subscribing papers published some, if not all, of the *Fuchsenfabeln,* and each of these papers was also regularly smuggled into Germany. It is impossible to ascertain the full impact of the fables on readers within Nazi Germany. But the editors of the *Deutsche Briefe* did receive a number of letters from within the Reich telling them at least that copies of the *Fuchsenfabeln* were being circulated. Knab recalls that this clandestine circulation was often increased by readers retyping the material and passing on more and more copies to others.

5

[5] Knab, *Interview.*

6

[6] Adolf Hitler, *My New Order,* edited by Raoul de Roussy de Sales (New York: Reynal & Hitchcock, 1941), p. 274.

7

[7] Knab, *Interview.* Knab also recalls a conversation with Gurian in which they agreed not to attack the Wehrmacht directly as long as there was even a faint hope that it might resist Hitler.

8

[8] In the course of my interview with Mr. Knab, he expressed amusement at his oversight, especially since he was unaware of it until the matter came up for discussion. Knab had heard the story about Göring being given a prize bull as a gift from the Russians, and on the train ride from Lucerne to Walchwil he toyed with the possibility of incorporating it somehow into the fables. He decided that he could very nicely squeeze a short little fable about the bull incident into a very small space on the *Deutsche Briefe* stencil and proceeded to do so. He felt the fable would fit into the scheme of the whole by pointing up the parallels between Nazism and Bolshevism.

9

[9] I have, quite obviously, not undertaken a judicious, historical analysis of the *Fuchsenfabeln* in this study. They have been treated in these pages largely as a body of literature of enduring quality. But appended to the translation of the fables that follow is a series of explanatory notes that will serve to clarify some of the specific historical references that the incidents in the fables parody, or parallel.

# CHAPTER THREE

# FUCHSENFABELN

## 1.

### Fox and the Foxes[1]

Once upon a time there was a fox. He did not do as other foxes do. He did not learn the crafts natural to his kind, and he did not want to live like the rest of his brothers. He felt himself born to higher things. Since, however, he could not recruit any sympathy for his notions in his local fox burrow, he ran away to his relatives.

Now, as Fox grew a bit older, his sentiments keeping pace with his increasing years, he one day gathered around him the foxes whom he knew and spoke to them as follows.

"My brothers! We are of the same kind, of the same color. Our pelts

---

[1] The fables have been numbered for the convenience of readers. When originally published, the fables were unnumbered.

are red, and fox's blood flows in our veins. We are a noble race. Indeed, we are the noblest. For in us the cleverness of our ancestors is bound together with the power of our limbs and the vigor of our bite. Indeed, in us, strength and intelligence are united. We are considered the very model of cunning, and we are famous as the champions of tenacity. We are heroes! Each and every one of us is a hero! Yet why, my brothers, why, my foxes, are we not what we ought to be in accordance with our virtues and in accordance with the plan of creation? Why are we not the leaders among the races of the earth? Because each one uses his cleverness, his strength, and his tenacity to pursue his own selfish interests. Because each one expends his ability on himself and nothing is left over for the whole—for the mass— for foxdom! But only think, my brothers! If each and every one of you is already so clever, so beautiful, so strong, so marvelous—think how clever and beautiful, how strong and noble, how marvelous we could be if we would merge our individual virtues into one, single virtue—the power and magnificence of our vulpine race! And do you, my beloved fellow foxes, understand what will be necessary to bring this about? We must become one! We must have one will—one, single will—the will of the foxes! No one may cling to his own selfish will; that would be treason! Away with the disgraceful intellect of certain foxes which has maneuvered our race into a dishonorable, undignified position! No fox has a right to his own private cleverness, to his own personal ability. Only the fox community can be the bearer of the fox identity, the fox virtue, and the fox heroic spirit. Away with the disgusting individual will which has destroyed the accomplishments of our race. One single will must inspire all of us. This will is the summation of all our race's noblest strivings and accomplishments. In me, my foxes, is embodied the individual will of each and every one of you. In me is embodied the strength and ability of our race that is so proud of its ancestry. I am your leader! I am your future! I am you! He who has genuine fox-blood flowing in his veins will believe in me. But he who does not believe in me has thereby demonstrated that he is no fox at all— for otherwise, he would believe in me! And he has further demonstrated that foreign, adulterated, profane blood flows through him, and he thereby expels himself from our community. He, however, who does believe in me will not go wrong. Even if I do not constantly conduct myself like a fox, I am still always a fox! Yes, even if I must clothe myself in the hide of our enemies, I remain a fox, for it is only in order to destroy our enemies that I disguise myself in their skin and that I speak their language. This is fox-cunning the like of which the world has never seen! This is fox-loyalty, for loyalty too is but a trick of my cunning! You, however, my foxes, I shall lead to a new day. In the most distant of days one will still glorify this time, for I shall lead you toward the millenium—the eternal millenium of foxes!"

Fox had finished. He stood there, the greatest fox of all time. With lightning suddenness his listeners took all his words into account.

"What? Whoever does not follow him is no longer a fox?"

"I am a fox!"

"I also."

"And I."

"And I."

And so there arose a mighty uproar from them, and from one end to another, Fox walked among his rejoicing, jubilant multitude.

---

## 2.

## The Ostrich, Fox, and, Then Again, the Ostrich

In his zoo, Sir Ostrich was attending a footrace of gentlemanly young ostriches when news of Fox's plan first reached him. He immediately reacted by disdainfully raising his high-held head. But when he discovered that quite a number of foxes were following in the tracks of the Great Fox, he assumed the proper attitude for an ostrich and high-stepped it over to the Great One's. On the way he considered the fact that Fox was not exactly a friend of birds, albeit he was fond of fowl, and Sir Ostrich thought he could take advantage of this. For first of all, he himself could only with certain qualifications be considered a fowl. Consequently the other birds did not so much love him as look up to him in awe. Secondly, remembering several occasions of disrespect among the chickens, Sir Ostrich perceived here a fine opportunity to teach, with Fox's help, the baser fowl some lessons in respect. So without further ado, he proposed to Fox, "Make me the supreme fowl in the land, and I will guarantee you supreme power over all the others."

Fox aimed a quick glance at the bare neck of the high-born gentleman, and thought to himself, "If need be, I can always risk a jump in that direction," and he nodded his approval of the proposition.

Then the ostrich presented Fox with a series of splendid projects. Fox took notice, selected what might be useful to him, and chose in such a manner that he succeeded in playing up to Sir Ostrich's vanity while always managing to look out for himself as well.

For a few months he let the ostrich enjoy his new role, and after the bird had finished his assignment and delivered the fowl to Fox, the Great One sent the ostrich packing. Sir Ostrich, of course, protested! He cited his rank. He cited his merits! But Fox only glanced upward in the direction of the high-born gentleman's naked neck. Then Sir Ostrich remembered why he had received long legs—in order to run. And he made use of them.

Now he stands aside and, as ostriches are wont to do, buries his head in the sand. And in this manner he celebrates Fox blindly and without the honors he had dreamed of, but the one—to be the noble servant of an ordinary fox . . . oh, and one more—to be Fox's court supplier of fowl.

23

### 3.

### Stewings and Doings among the Feathered-Folk

About the time when word got around that Fox was planning to take over control of the entire animal kingdom, the feathered-folk, who were understandably disturbed, gathered in conference. They debated excitedly. They formed committees and subcommittees. They assigned committee reporters. Some of the assembled counseled for unified resistance, but that would have endangered the peace, and the pacifists among them could not possibly accede to that. They rather tended to the opinion that war was immoral under all circumstances, and morality demanded that it would be better to let themselves be strangled and eaten, than to defend themselves and in the process of defending themselves risk hurting the poor aggressor. A rather strong group advocated letting Fox have his own will—to let him take on the responsibility for leadership while they would remain in passive resistance. Then, they argued, Fox's megalomania would soon come to naught. For what, after all, would such a mammal understand of the ways of birds and fishes, or even the amphibious animals? What indeed! In this way the danger could be overcome in the easiest way, by simply driving out the Devil with Beelzebub. "If he himself doesn't have a devil in him," cracked a wise, old marabou calmly. But, of course, all of the assembled, living as they were in an enlightened age, simply smiled over the joke.

At last the conference was postponed until the experts might work out a proposal outlining what steps should be taken next, and then they could always get together to consult about the results. After all, Fox's plan was at best utopian, and if worst came to worst, they had recourse to a long tradition of experience against which these ill-bred opponents would have no chance.

And then it happened that somewhere in foxdom one of Fox's burrows collapsed.

"Sabotage!" cried the Great Fox. "The animal kingdom is in danger! We must save it!" And he leaped at the first frightened fowl he saw and bit clear through his neck. Excitedly the frightened birds flew in all directions, some directly into the mouths of the lurking foxes. And the vulpines' teeth started grinding. But the birds who managed to remain unscathed applauded with their wings as if they rejoiced in their savior. But they did so only to escape the vulpines' deadly bite. And they were immensely relieved when they could return to their nests, their feathers intact.

"See," said the Great Fox that evening to his followers, "this is the fruit of our daring. Now the feathered-folk also praise and welcome me. They thank us that we have liberated them from their leaders who planned only to sow distrust between us. Now they all love us; all those whom we have today saved, or at least spared."

4.

## The Cardinal and the Birdlover

The cardinal was a high-ranking bird. Because he possessed such dignity, he fancied he could impress the victorious Fox. He flew over to a branch under which Fox was resting and began singing to him that he was ready to negotiate. In front of Fox's burrow, however, hung some cages, a great many cages in fact, in which all kinds of roughed-up feathery-folk squatted dispiritedly behind bars. The cardinal was of course disturbed by what he saw, and he inquired of Fox why he kept so many of the birds as prisoners. Fox assumed a very sad countenance, as though it were his lot to be everywhere misunderstood, and he said, "Prisoners you say? Well, am I then a torturer of animals? Do I look like a torturer? What do you take me to be, my dear friend? I am a friend of the birds. Indeed, I am a birdlover! Just look at the poor wretches. Did they ever have it so good in their lives, as right here and now under my hospitality? They have everything they need. In fact, they have more than they need. All I do here is condition them to the new times, times which they could otherwise not tolerate, in which they would surely perish. They are here for their own protection, in order to be educated to become . . ."

". . . meals," thought Fox's jailor, who was listening close by.

But aloud his master said, ". . . useful members of our community."

At these words the cardinal ruffled his feathers and let it be known that this was why he was here: in order to assure Fox that the community of birds was freely willing to cooperate with Fox's new community. He himself and all the birds had, after all, always advocated the notion of community. Fox asserted that nothing was more welcome to his ears than to hear this. The cardinal, he continued, could be assured that his community would be freely welcomed into the empire of the foxes if only they would now sing their amens to the greater glory of Fox's power.

Then the cardinal flew down to the lowest branch of the tree and whistled his personal amen loudly in front of all the cages. At this, Fox arose, pleased and happy. And now the cardinal received a royal handshake. (It must be said, however, that the royal paw was still somewhat sticky from the last and quite recent bird meal.) But with a flutter of his wings the cardinal departed. As soon as he had a few bird-miles between himself and Fox, he shook himself, preened his feathers, smoothed back his plume, cleaned his glasses until they shone, tidied up his hands, and then flew off across the mountains. There, far from the empire of Fox and his cages, he warbles and warbles up to this very day, "He has shaken hands with me! He is a gentleman! And he has promised me . . . what exactly has he promised, this Fox? Oh, so what! He has shaken hands with me!"

## 5.

### The Feeding

"Peep," complained a sparrow. He was hungry.

"Peep, peep!" The imploring chirp came from all the cages.

"Here you do not act in your old, humdrum ways," ranted Fox. "Here we do not say 'peep,' we say 'zeeg!'" ·

The birds were silent. After a little while a green finch gave it a try. "Zeeg." Immediately he was handed a crumb of bread. "Zeeg, zeeg!" he chirped in thanks, and he was in turn further rewarded with a few fingerfuls.

"Zeeg, zeeg, zeeg!" came the cry from all over. In response Fox threw a few pawfuls of birdseed into the cages, and laughing, walked away.

The game appealed to the pettier foxes. All over the country they posted themselves around the feeding places of the birds, wherever they knew the hungry ones must come, and kept the morsels from those who did not first loudly proclaim, "Zeeg! Zeeg!" True, some of the birds stood stubbornly aside. These became ever thinner, paler, and weaker. But finally, when their young ones started crying, they too blurted out, "Zeeg! Zeeg!" This provided the foxes with a good laugh.

"Our Fox is indeed a shrewd fellow," they said among themselves. "How simple it is to rule." They did not let up with their game: first "Zeeg!" then feed; first bow, then chow. "They must learn to eat out of our hands," said the foxes.

"Zeeg! Zeeg! Zeeg!"

The cry resounded throughout the land.

## 6.

### The Weasel

One day Fox summoned the weasel.

"Old friend," Fox began, "I have a job for you. Understand, it is a very special assignment. You can insure my favor by bringing it off, so listen. I have here a very irksome contract. The cardinal—you know, the one who flew the coop across the mountains—well, I made—how shall I say it—a sort of gentleman's agreement with him, all notarized and very solemn, you know, complete with signature and seal. You understand."

"I understand," grumbled the weasel, "but where do I . . ."

"Slowly, slowly, old soldier," said Fox. "Here is the situation. This thing, this contract, must be kept."

"Kept?" wondered the weasel in surprise.

"Yes, it must be kept," continued Fox, "a question of prestige. So for the time being I'll have to do without fowl on my table. Well, let them cluck, that is all they can do anyway. But now listen carefully. In that particular black nest I already told you about, there are some 'contractual eggs,' you understand? Very fragile things, but very important. Extremely important! Don't ever break any of those eggs! Not one! Only—and now I will tell you why I sent for you—you are of course a specialist in the treatment of eggs."

"Ah!" The weasel was beginning to enjoy himself. "Now I understand what you mean. Sucking?"

Fox nodded. "Yes, sucking! That and nothing more. Suck them dry, until there is nothing—but nothing—left in them. But I can allow you only one tiny hole for each egg, so tiny that it will remain undetected as long as possible. And the eggs must stay where they are, even when they are empty, as long as I want them to. Understand?"

In response the weasel wrinkled his brow so that his eyes became mere slits. "It will be done," he said. But in a regretful tone he added, "And all those many beautiful throats?"

"Later, later. Only be patient," replied Fox.

---

## 7.

### How Fox Encountered the Various Animals

Fox scurried through the land and looked about him. He observed how all the birds trembled before him in awe and he marveled at how easy it had been to manage this with only a few cages.

"All great things are simple to achieve," he said to the foxes that accompanied him. "The secret is only this: to do what others dare not do and to blame those others for what one has himself done."

"How wise he is," admired his companions. But Fox continued to address them.

"I have taken you with me so that you may become my co-workers. The empire of the foxes is entrusted to you. Everything I do, I do for you. You should learn to enjoy it. But to enjoy means to rule and to rule means also to be on guard. For this reason we cannot allow the other animals to unite. Instead we must make our own separate agreements with each of the species. We shall be dignified with the dignified, great with the great, and low with the lowly. In such a way we will cultivate friends in all of the species. And these, our new friends, will rule more effectively and more jealously than we alone would be able to do. I will prove that to you."

While he was thus speaking, he came upon a field where a flock of sheep, guarded by a black dog, was grazing. Fox inched closer to the grazing animals. They ran from the stranger, helter skelter, bumping into each other, and off again in all directions, not knowing at all how they should behave.

"You are such useful subjects in my empire," Fox called to them. "I know that you are loyal and peaceful and that you always do your duty. You have for a long time commanded my affection. But I can see that you need protection to insure order among yourselves." He signaled the strapping, black dog to come to him. Fox looked him over, was pleased with what he saw, and said to him, "I like you, fellow. I like your insolence. Gather together the biggest and strongest of your kind and come to work for me, all of you. Right now you are only dogs, but I will make rulers of you. You shall be my bodyguards and you shall also keep watch over the flocks of my empire."

He then turned from them and walked along beside a brook where he found a rich hamster sitting, keeping guard over his treasures. Fox addressed him, "My friend, you are indispensable to the empire of the animals. But you live here in fear of those who are greedy for your riches. I'll make you a proposition which will free you from all your worries: give me what I need and I will keep a tight rein on all those whom you fear." All the foxes' eyes gleamed as Fox spoke these words, and the hamster, delighted with the generous offer, signed the contract mouthing a thousand words of thanks.

The Great Fox continued on through the land.

"I will have the cattle in my land protected like the sheep," he explained to his companions. "I will turn over the horses, the donkeys, and even the pigs to the care of my dogs who will be loyal to me because they are allowed to rule."

"But what about man who is supposed to be so much cleverer than we? What if he lures these animals away from us?" ventured one of the smallest foxes. The other foxes chimed in, "Yes, what about the great men?"

But Fox cut them short. "Who is greater than I?" he countered. "Who is more clever? I will show you how powerful I am. I will watch over man by means of the lowest creatures in my empire, by means of the tiniest insect." Fox sniffed the air about him and in one, calculated maneuver caught himself a gnat. "This one," he said, "this one and her sisters the flies, and her brothers the bugs, and their kinsmen from the fleas to the ticks I will use as my police, my secret police, whom I will set on the heels of men. And then I will know all that they say in council and I will be able to undo everything."

The other foxes were astounded at their leader's intellect. They continued on, still overawed, when they chanced upon a knotted clump of snakes. These slithered up out of the grass and hissed, "You are entering a mighty kingdom. This is the home of the old lion."

At this warning, Fox bowed reverently and said to the king's messengers, "Tell your master I greet him. I am proud that he spreads his splendor in my domain. May he always feel welcome in the forest of the foxes." Having thus extended his regards, he turned from the snakes and smilingly addressed his companions. "This is perhaps the greatest skill of all: to allow certain dangerous animals the illusion that they make fools of us. It is only in this way that we can in the end make fools of them."

And this Fox has done to this very day.

8.

## The Parrot Plague

Jako, the gray parrot, the most famous speechmaker among his kind, he who had long trumpeted the Great Fox's fame all over the world, was silent. He was silent for a long time because he was thinking. And when he had finished thinking, he fluttered awkwardly—for the Creator endowed parrots more for climbing than for flying—over to the Great Fox-burrow, and there he had himself announced.

"It is good that you have come," Fox called out to him. "I have a job for you."

"Great Fox, our thoughts are running on the same track," said the gray one. "I, too, have a plan."

"How often have I told you," began Fox, "that our nation of foxes can have only one will?"

Jako nodded, "Your will, of course."

"Idiot bird!" Fox retorted angrily. "Not *my* will, the foxes' will!"

"The foxes' will," parroted Jako, "the will of all foxes."

"That's more like it!" bristled Fox. He kept to himself for awhile until his anger subsided, then blurted out, "But so that all will come to know just what their will really is, it is imperative to tell them what it is they want."

"Wise one," replied Jako, "my stupidity has profited from your wisdom. I have entertained a similar thought."

After Fox and Jako had sat and talked in this way for some time, the parrot fluttered away and began traveling from forest to forest, from park to park, starting one parrot school after another. In these schools dozens, hundreds, thousands, tens of thousands of rather limited parrots suddenly learned to speak a new language. They learned it as no speakers had ever learned a language before. And when their heads and hearts were filled to the brim, they flew out into the land. There their sharp beaks overflowed with what they had to say and the words dripped from their tireless, flapping tongues, flooding all creation, flowing through fields, forests, valleys, mountains, cities, villages, even to the remotest hamlet, inundating men and beasts alike; thousands, tens of thousands, hundreds of thousands, millions, dozens of millions of parrots, so that no one could save himself from this unrestrained horde who prattled and prated, chattered and clattered, and blustered and swarmed in all directions, until there was nowhere even the smallest spot left where one could find relief from the interminable racket.

"We want!" they shrieked. "We want! We want!"

And whenever between breaths a few confused and half-demented ones started asking, "What do we want?" the others drowned out the questioners with new cries of "We want! We want! We want what he wants—the one who thinks and wills for us all—the Great Fox!"

The air was filled with the shriek of parrots. And the eyes of all other creatures were blinded, for those who shrieked were splendidly attired in glittering colors. Then the parrots carried their pomp and power into all the world.

"We are parrots, we are parrots!" they shrieked. "We will make the entire world into parrots!"

## 9.

### How the Fishes Were Rewarded

In these same days, it happened that a great honor was paid to the fishes.  The Great Fox in person visited the waters of his land.  He allowed his yellow foxes to march in review and his black dogs to pass in festive parade.  Then he ordered them to stand at attention.  And in the breathless quiet of the moment he proclaimed to the fishes, "My dear fishes, I have come to realize that you are the most useful subjects in my empire.  For you are voiceless.  In order to pay you my respects and to express to you my thanks, I herewith solemnly proclaim you as examples for our nation.  May my entire people become as you are.  Among you there are no grumblers, no defeatists, no critics.  You serve the community by being quietly, wordlessly willing to be devoured.  Hail to you, my dumb countrymen!"

"Zeeg! Zeeg!" yelled Fox's soldiers.

The fishes, however, only gave fresh evidence of their virtue.  They tolerated even this, and remained dumb.

## 10.

### Schoolmaster Fly and the Cuckoo Parents

"I intend to implant my knowledge in all the descendants of my empire." So spoke the Great Fox one day to his cohorts. He knew he could count on them to inculcate in their children every day and every hour what he, Fox, had taught them, and that they would feed his teachings to their little ones in every drop of fox-mothers' milk. But since he himself had no descendants (he had had to spend all of his time in thinking and making decisions, and therefore never had a minute to reproduce his own), he summoned the ichneumon flies and the cuckoos to appear before him. He spoke to them as follows.

"I intend to favor you, my loyal ones, with a very special kindness. I have selected you to guarantee the everlastingness of my empire. I know that no one in the empire of animals can stand against me because they fear my bite and my claws. And because they fear me, they adhere to me with their devotion. However, I am also aware that among the older animals, who now sing my praises, there are many secret enemies who are envious of our victory and who are waiting only for us to slip and stumble on some stupidity. We have the right to make our own mistakes, but we will not fall over them. We will rather build upon them. These enemies, however, believe they can destroy us by withholding their children from us. This we must prevent. I have chosen you, my trusted cuckoos, my loyal flies, to perform this task."

"Zeeg! Zeeg!" they yelled joyously.

"You see," continued Fox, "I could issue a law which would compel all the young to be surrendered to me. I could take them from all those parents who do not please me. I could do all this because I have the power to do so. However, I choose not to do this because I am generous! Nonetheless, I am responsible to see to it that the youth of my nation do not succumb to the errors of their elders. And for that reason, I have resolved on an especially noble deed which is in keeping with my generosity. I will honor my enemies by allowing them to bring up my own offspring! But you, my loyal ones, will go out and imbue yourselves with my spirit and my doctrines even more thoroughly than you have done in the past. And when you have been sufficiently filled with them, follow your own natural ways and begin working for me. You flies will go forth and select the appropriate elements in the land and implant into their bodies the seed from which the new life as we envision it will grow to see the light. And their elders, with their own strength and blood, will nourish the very thing they want to destroy—our brood. However, you, my cuckoos, after you have filled yourselves with the knowledge of my will, will go out and lay your eggs into the nests of all those in the land who secretly oppose me. Then these insubordinates will hatch and rear *our* descendants, *our* youth! And thus, my cuckoos, you will be the parents of these youths in my place. The state's parents of my state's youth! And to you flies, I will also entrust the schooling of these youths. You will not, as the schoolmasters of old, teach with loud speeches. My parrots will do that. Quietly and without drawing attention, you will, while my parrots do the speechmaking, sow your seed among those whom we will conquer with their own offspring. And no one shall see you doing it! For now you must work in the night. But one day in the future you will be able to announce in the light of your efforts, 'We have created anew the race of our empire!' "

Then the flies and cuckoos flew away and did exactly as they were told. Soon the oldest among the elders got together and shook their heads in dismay. For they had noticed that at the time when their young ones were hardly yet able to speak, when their mothers took them on their laps in order to teach them their first prayers, the little ones laughed in their faces and yelled, "Zeeg! Zeeg!" But the council of elders had no solution and they were without any power to act. The oldest of the elders spoke up.

"No principle of our life has been touched. The family has been retained. It is, then, from the family that improvement must come. Let us thank the Great Fox for having saved the family and for having made it the foundation of his empire."

Little did they realize that the family had been hollowed out, just as the weasels had hollowed out the eggs in accordance with the will of the Great Fox.

They praised the Great Fox!

**11.**

## The Wise Owls

One night, after the summons of the Great Fox had reached them, the wise owls congregated in a crumbling old building. The screech owls haughtily surveyed the wise company and pushed their way arrogantly through rows of respectable barn owls who, out of the slits of their eyes, looked suspiciously about sizing up their colleagues and the entire company. Suddenly the long, drawn-out "ooohooo, ooohooo" of Bubu the eagle owl silenced all conversation, and he soared over the wise gathering on soundless wings. Everyone remained silent, for Bubu was a confidant of the Great Fox, entrusted with supervising all learning in the fox empire. Now the powerful one seated himself upon a raised stone behind a row of snappy young foxes who had marched in and he began to address the assembly in a loud voice.

"The empire of the animals through the spirit, courage, and power of the Great Fox has at last been liberated from the chains of traditional prejudices. Thus, the night of liberation has also arrived for science and scholarship." With eyes agleam he shot a glance toward a group of owls seated around a table. "All too long a certain, intellectually contaminated element of day-shy scholars has presumed to serve a wholly misunderstood idea of learning with the mere accumulation of knowledge. And they were not ashamed to teach and conduct their research with what they chose to call objectivity. Only when the Great Fox, uneducated and unspoiled creature of nature that he is, stepped in to make the redeeming pronouncement 'We are subjects and therefore life is subjective,' was it realized that scholarship has the duty to search out and teach, not what serves all, but only what serves the greatness, the splendor, the dignity, and the perfection of the vulpine race. Learning can no longer be allowed to proceed in the criminal objectivity of the past. No longer may anyone dare to analyze so-called errors with their scholarly hocus-pocus. It lies in the very nature of the most noble of all races that erroneous ideas, mistakes, and imperfections simply do not exist; that every so-called error that is discovered is only the proof of the error and inability of certain scholars.

"What, then, have you gentlemen accomplished?" Bubu cried out. "What have you done for the great empire of foxes? You have done nothing! You have been sitting in your ivory towers cooing to your secluded selves while others have been struggling to build the new empire with tooth and claw. Prove to us then that you are not mere deadwood in the empire of the Great Fox. Scholarship has been handed a new task in foxdom. You may prove what the will of the people affirms. You may lay a scholarly foundation for what the energy of the Great Fox produces in accomplished deeds. You may research the sources in which alone lie all the error and guilt of the past. You may investigate the evil-smelling sources of corruption, refuse, and crime which alone have for so long prevented Fox from proclaiming to the world his new insights, the insights of his intellect. This, my dear owls," concluded Bubu, "is your task: mold the magnificent thoughts and ideas of the Great Fox into a system so that the world may recover its health in the new fox philosophy of our millenium of foxes!"

The screech owls broke into noisy applause. The foxes in front of the speaker's platform stamped their feet in approval so vigorously that the crumbling fragments from the walls of the old scholarship rained down on them. And then great numbers of owls began clamoring for the chance to be heard. The wise assembly began to speak, to write, and to lecture so furiously that the meeting was soon transformed into pedagogic pandemonium. Every one of the owls uncovered a system of his own which proved conclusively that his teaching had never been anything else than the great prophecy which had now been fulfilled. Indeed, they discovered (with all the modesty that had, of course, always characterized their scholarly endeavors) that they could point to themselves as the pioneers of the Great Fox *Weltanschauung* and of the fox philosophy of world domination. What is more, they discovered that without their pioneering work, the world would have had to wait another millenium for the arrival of the Great Fox.

Bubu smiled knowingly out over his audience. "You have grasped the times, my colleagues."

37

## 12.

### The Envy of the Woodpeckers

It happened, however, that the owls' unanimous adoption of the new fox-learning manifested itself more and more in all the academic literature, pervading all aspects of it to such an extent that the woodpeckers turned yellow and green with envy. Even the black woodpeckers started to take on various, unfamiliar, bright colors, while brooding over how they could outdo the superwise owls. They therefore began a great hammering in the forests and gardens of the land which sounded like a proclamation for battle. The conifer underworld, bugs, larvae, and insects of every kind, lived through anxious days. Soon, though, they realized that this time the hammering was not directed against them, but that instead, the noble woodpeckers were busily engaged in hammering out hour-long memoranda.

The Great Fox, lord of the fields and forests, had recently spoken with great derision of the old, outmoded, corrupted, and politicized form of justice, and he had demanded a new justice. Hence this army of woodpeckers, the jurists of the forest, was now at work hammering together a new body of law. Splinters of unusable codes fell by the wayside, each one hammered out more furiously than the last, when on a morning radiant with the brightness of sunny fox-weather the Great Fox hurried through the woods hearing the "Zeeg" calls of the woodpeckers reverberate through all the tree trunks in the forest.

Arriving on the scene the Great One summoned all the woodpeckers around him, and letting them first wait a goodly while before he began, he assumed a darkened mien and said, "I hate the jurists!"

"Zeeg!" they all yelled, for they were delighted with his frankness.

"I hate justice," he continued. "The jurists with their unfoxlike justice had almost become the gravediggers of my future and would have if I had not set my law, the coming new law, against your law, gentlemen," here Fox grimaced, "and had not your justice been so miserably objective and so weakly humane that it thereby allowed me to slip through the meshes of its nets. But now there will be no more of this light-headed humanitarianism. Now I will determine what is right. None of you, my gentlemen jurists, will in the future be able to pronounce, formulate, or appeal to any kind of law unless he can refer it to my will and thereby fulfill my will. Because, gentlemen, the will of the people is manifested in me! And the law of the people is embodied in me! Justice, however, is only that which will serve the purpose of the fox empire. Crime is what undermines our purpose! Take note, gentlemen, and act accordingly! If I institute anything for which you have no legal codes, then create these codes! If I reject anything for which there is no precedent in your laws, make precedents! That is why you are jurists. You must be enforcers of my will! That means you must be the executors of the will of our great, superior nation of foxes! Earn this honor, gentlemen!"

Fox paused for a moment to clear his throat. Then he continued, "You have here produced a mountain of memoranda, analyses, and expert opinions. I do not want to see them. Hammer together whatever *I* will. That, and nothing else, is your duty!"

A tumultuous "Zeeg!" arose from the woodpeckers and one black woodpecker, a professor of law, stood up joyfully and shouted loudly above the approving din, "The will of Fox is the supreme law! Fox protects the law!"

Hearing these words, the Great Fox was moved to graciousness. He then pronounced the historic words, "Now you have realized that I am the supreme judge of all. Up to this moment you have only judged criminals. I, however, will give you tasty morsels to digest!"

**13.**

## "Fuchs, Du hast . . ."

It was six days after the summer solstice had been celebrated in the empire of Fox.  In the forest a red and a black grouse were playing together, not giving a thought to anything as they sang into the beautiful day, with a truly resounding warble, "Fuchs, Du hast die Gans gestohlen, gib sie wieder her . . ." ("Fox, you've gone and stole the goose, give it back again . . .").

Now it so happened that the Great Fox was at this very moment returning through the forest from his meeting with the woodpeckers when the sound of the treasonous song reached him.  He ordered his companions to stay behind, and taking along his bodyguard, stealthily approached the singing.  Then he saw the unsuspecting grouse who were romping amorously in the grass, and for diversion were amusing themselves by digging up a few worms and torturing them much as they had seen the foxes torment their prisoners.  The two had just begun again to accompany their sport with another chorus of "Fuchs, Du hast . . ." when out of nowhere a red shadow leaped upon them—then a second one.  The grouse never even fluttered their wings, so quickly were they scrunched between the foxes' teeth!  Blood oozed from the attackers' mouths.  Then the Great Fox plunked the still warm meat onto the moss, licked his snout, and snapped to his bodyguard, "Run to the Fox-burrow . . . run!  Release the black dogs.  I will it!  The grouse have planned an uprising against me!  Get rid of them!  All of them!"

The bodyguard, grinning from ear to ear at the command, had already turned on his heels to go, when he turned back once more and asked, "Why only grouse, Great Fox? Aren't there more fowl who don't love us? A few black crows maybe? A few white geese? Some juicy chickens?"

"Eat them!" yelled Fox. "Devour them! Devour them!"

When Fox returned home he surveyed the execution. He was not able any more to tally all the victims. But there were many. By mistake even a few parrots had been slaughtered. But, after all, there was enough of their kind left, and that was the important thing.

"Do you command the woodpeckers, Sir?" Fox was asked by an associate. But he only motioned him away. Suddenly he yelled wildly, "I am my own woodpecker! I am my own parrot! I am my own bloodhound! I am everything I want to be!" Then he ran over to the assembled gathering and screamed, "I am your liberator! I have freed you from the beasts! I am your savior! For I could have destroyed you but I have kept you in reserve. I am a hero because I have had my fill!"

Then throughout the land the animals put their heads together and turned around cautiously, as if looking for someone or something . . . they did not know what. They perked up their ears to hear some sound, but heard nothing. There was no one left who dared to sing "Fuchs, Du hast . . . ."

But all the creeping, crawling, running, and flying predators of the forest assembled around the Great Fox. Among them was the butcherbird, whom everyone called a mockingbird because he had the ability to mimic the voices of numerous other birds and thereby lure them to his trap. He was installed as head of the Great Fox's secret police.

And now the Great Fox was more powerful than ever before.

**14.**

## The Much-Traveled Bison

The bison had made a very long journey. He had been born far away in the Russian Caucasus, but since a certain high official in the fox empire had longed to own such a bison bull, he was allowed to make a long railroad journey which took him thousands of miles into a northern heath. There the master of the hunt who had so wanted the bull came on his first visit to see him. The high official looked the beautiful animal over approvingly and loved him at first sight. He addressed him with these words.

"You have come from far off, my friend."

The bison was silent.

"How powerful you are and how defiant in the strength of your natural beauty!"

The bison was silent.

"You are wild, untameable, and unpredictable in your raging strength."

The bison was silent.

"Those crafty, treacherous eyes—they make you quite impenetrable, you know."

The bison was silent.

"You are like me," continued the keeper. "You are a picture of my own nature!"

Hearing this the bison spoke just six words.

"Yes, I am also a Bolshevik."

Then he was again silent.

The foxes, however, and the parrots were not admitted to the heath where the bison made his residence. Had they been admitted, they might well have noticed what the bull was . . . and perhaps, just possibly, he might even have talked once more.

## 15.

## The Migratory Birds Begin Their Travels

One morning, as the traveling season drew nigh in the fox empire, the parrots swarmed out into all the corners of the land on a great recruiting campaign.

"Stay at home, brother birds," they clattered, "if you value your lives! Over there in the land of the winter sun the bird-catchers will be waiting to snare you for the roasting spits, for they wish to annihilate us all. But here in the empire of Fox you enjoy limitless security. And to set an example, we too will stay at home." (The parrots, of course, lived in centrally heated villas, and never had a worry or a care about being regularly fed.) "The Great Fox," they continued, "will arrange his own special, guided tours of the fabulous scenic wonders of our winterland which will take your minds off the material pleasures of ordinary insect hunts. And thus you will learn to gain strength through joy."

But the migratory birds thought to themselves, "We'd better get out while the going's good!" So they took off over the heads of the envious ones who also longed to go, but had to stay behind. And they flew high over the passes of the fox empire into other lands where the fishes had not yet been made the examples for all the animal kingdom. Several wild geese and wild ducks also accompanied the migratory birds, and these had no intention of returning to the nests in their homeland so long as they knew them to be within reach of Fox and his followers. When the parrots got wind of this, they began to agitate against that unpatriotic rabble of emigrant birds, and wherever anything went wrong in the empire, the emigrant birds were made the scapegoats and their nests were duly confiscated.

And when the animals in other lands began to be suspicious and even hostile toward the Great Fox, whose strange actions they had begun to notice, Fox mounted a podium and thundered, "I have never declared otherwise than that I love everyone so much that I could eat them all! But that lying emigrant pack of wild geese and ducks honks and quacks it about the world that I devour out of greed, while in fact I do so only out of pure love!"

But time passed and once again the sun returned to the fox empire. The migratory birds returned to their homesteads in the fields. Many a one, however, was snatched up and dragged before the courts by the predatory birds, the hawks, falcons, and buzzards, who had been recruited into Fox's secret service. For some of the returnees had not been discreet enough in the warmer countries they had visited; they had been unaware that quite a few vermin had secretly tucked themselves into their feathers and had spied on all their doings. Now they had to undertake another kind of journey, one less free and not of their choosing. Their wings were clipped so that they were unable to fly any more. Now they could only flutter feebly to and fro, always within reach of the foxes' teeth, the dogs' bite, or the talons of the secret police. That was the punishment for their frivolity.

In the meantime some exotic vacationers from the warmer areas of the world had journeyed with the stream of returning birds into the fox empire. Foremost among them were some wealthy cranes and some very aristocratic herons. They took up residence at the fashionable spas of the Baltic and North Seas, and also populated the mountain retreats. Occasionally they had heard frightful tales and even some atrocity stories from the migratory birds about the Great Fox's regime. But now, after a quick look around, they decided that it had all been a great lie; they did not see one corpse lying in the streets or public squares. The Great Fox was rumored to have murdered. But now, as always before, there were fish delicacies and the most exquisitely seasoned froglegs on the menus. Fox was said to terrorize the inhabitants of his empire. But one needed only to stroll down the streets to meet everywhere laughing foxes and well-groomed dogs. The noblest predators cruised through the air and the sporting life of the seagulls was, if anything, livelier than ever. And if one cared to do a little slumming down in the swamps and marshes, one could still do it as well as in the old days—perhaps even better, for there was less annoyance from the common rabble. And even the ordinary chickens were going about their business, mating and multiplying.

And so these travelers returned to their homelands and announced, "Look how the Great Fox maintains flawless order! Come and see!"

## 16.

## Reporter Stork Goes Interviewing

There was no more denying it. The world was uneasy. The empire of Fox, however far it had reached, did, after all, have its boundaries. And the neighbors behind these boundaries had picked up a suspicious scent. What their noses told them was that Fox was preparing for war. Now they thought amongst themselves, "If Fox enjoys wreaking havoc, let him do so among his own. That is a domestic matter in which we do not wish to become entangled. On the other hand, if his appetite should threaten us, then of course justice and civilization themselves would be in danger, and steps would have to be taken to meet this threat."

So they decided to find the matter out. They selected an internationally respected journalist for this purpose, one who was known to be objective and unprejudiced and who had few enemies. This was the stork, and he was sent abroad.

### Reporter Stork's First Interview

The stork first flew over to Jako, the gray parrot, the greatest speech-maker among all the parrots.

"What would you like to know?" asked the gray one engagingly. "Just ask!"

"Is it correct," began the stork, "that the great majority in your nation supports the regime of the Great Fox?"

Jako smiled. "One cannot fail to notice that you come from democratic regions. But I will be honest with you. It is, of course, not true."

"Well then, is . . ."

But the gray parrot had only made a rhetorical pause and now he finished his sentence. "The truth is rather that the totality of our animals stands behind the Great Fox! We have overcome the antiquated and pernicious concept of majority. Majority is only part. We work with the whole, the spirit of the whole, my good sir!"

"The last elections," the stork interrupted, "have nonetheless shown that a not entirely inconsequential minority is not in favor of the regime, your excellency."

"That was merely errors in counting, terribly exaggerated by international journalism," Jako countered in his deepest, most forebearing, and most paternal tone. "But our regime has unmasked these erroneous tallies as mistakes. And there was a small number of uneducated ones who, in the excitement and enthusiasm of the moment, made a slip of the pen. We have of course corrected these errors. So the final result does indeed reflect the real will of the nation. You know, surely, that we have only one will, the will of Fox?"

"Would that mean then," said the stork, "that those elements against which Fox was . . ."

Jako genially helped him along, "forced?"

"Naturally," hastened the stork, "forced to move. . . . Would this then mean that even these animals would today acknowledge Fox?"

"What does 'acknowledge' mean?" crackled Jako. "They all love, love— they revere him!"

The stork wrote everything down.

"They thank him," continued Jako, "for liberating them from the prejudices of their former erroneous ways. They revere him with a boundless gratitude because he has been generous as no fox before him was generous. He did not barbarically devour them as would have been his right, for he is, after all, the strongest. Instead he spared them. Indeed they actually worship him because he has become their fate, their providence, their destiny! And what it has never become the good fortune of our many religious organizations to achieve—the free and voluntary submission of an army of millions of creatures to one Godhead—our renewed nation in its totality has freely realized in the expression of its love for their great fox leader. And therefore we can say in all truth that the will of the Great Fox is the will of the nation. And the will of Fox is the will of God!"

"This was the essence of my question," said the stork. "The consensus in the fox empire then is no mere rumor, but. . ."

"Fact!" cried Jako. "Accomplished fact! And it is more. It is our dogma! It is our gospel!"

## Reporter Stork's Second Interview

The stork then flew over to the Great Fox himself. He asked to be announced and requested that he be allowed to seek answers to three questions. He was invited in and there he found the Great Fox busily reading the book he had written when he was not yet called the "Great Fox," but rather the "dumb fox." The Powerful One closed the book and laid it aside so that the stork could just make out the title: *My Struggle*. The Great Fox seated himself upon an outspread map which represented the world and which was his throne. Then the stork, responding to a soft, inviting gesture of Fox's paw, began to speak.

"Great Fox," he addressed him, "your fame has spread beyond the borders of your empire. Your name is mentioned with great esteem and admiration, but also with fear."

"Fear is only an imperfect form, a pre-stage so to speak, of love," said Fox quietly and thoughtfully. "Only he whom I have first liberated will ever love me."

The stork was somewhat confused but nonetheless opened his beak again and said, "My first question, Great Fox, is this. What is your view concerning the boundaries of your empire?"

"I do not even think of them. They do not even exist in my thoughts," replied Fox in great amazement and somewhat offended.

"I thank you, Great Fox," bowed the stork. He was pleased. "Then does it follow that you do not contemplate war, as is rumored by so many in neighboring lands? Do you then, and this is my second question, intend to keep the peace, Great Fox?"

"Keep? What a narrow concept!" replied Fox with dignity. "I love peace. My land has never known more peace than it has since the day when the race of foxes assumed its right to dominion. Tell it, write it, proclaim it to the world. I love peace so much that I instruct my entire nation, from the infants to the senile ones, in the use of weapons, only so that no one will ever dare to disturb our peace. Indeed I must say more. I love peace so much that I will carry it forth into the entire world for all time, so that nowhere will peace ever again be annihilated by war. Others have wanted peace. I, however, will realize it! And I will realize it because I will weld it to the honor of my great, noble, and superior race."

The stork was again confused, but he nevertheless formulated, with absolute correctness, his last question. "Great Fox, in your wisdom you have anticipated my third question. Wherein does the honor of the race of foxes consist, as you, Great Fox, proclaim and demand it for your empire?"

At that the Great Fox arose, splendid in his appearance, arranged his bushy red tail with dignity as if it were kingly ermine, and spoke as follows. "The world asks me about things which I have already told them. Here lies my book. Tell the world that they should read it! I have not renounced one, single word in it, nor do I intend to renounce one, single word. However, I will be generous and answer your question.

"Our race, the race of foxes, is the noblest race amongst all creatures. Ever since the establishment of my rule my scientists and scholars have with self-sacrificing devotion proven this fact irrefutably. However, it is the will of the Creator that the great must rule over the small, the superior over the inferior, the noble over the lowly. Our highest race contains within itself the natural right of domination over all inferior races. The race of the foxes is scattered over the countries of the world. Foxes' blood flows in the sable of Siberia and in the desert fox, the jackal of Africa. Foxes' blood flows in the prairie coyote and through the wolf of the Asian steppes. And even in the land of eternal ice, the eternally noble blood of our race triumphs in the blue-pelted Arctic fox. *Our blood knows no boundaries. Therefore, our right can know no boundaries. And neither will our will recognize any boundaries.* All struggle in the world is a war for the restoration of right order. This natural struggle will be ended on the day when the last race, the last nation, will, of its own free will, as the animals of my own empire have done, make good the injustices done to the race of the foxes, and will restore the honor of the fox by recognizing our right to world dominion! When the honor of foxes' blood is thus satisfied, then true peace will be restored, the peace of the foxes! And it will be eternal peace, to which we will everlastingly pledge ourselves!"

When the Great Fox had finished speaking in this manner, he called in one of his ministers and forthwith signed the Order for Mobilization for the Preservation of Peace.

Then the stork was dismissed.

## 17.

### The Conference of the Crows

News of the stork's interview and Fox's act of mobilizing his empire for the preservation of peace created a sensation which fell like a bomb onto the anxious world. The crows were hurriedly called from all corners of the world to an international conference because they were considered to be the most peaceful of all animals, and it was known of them that no one of them had ever scratched out the eye of another. And the world promised itself success from these proceedings.

So the crows gathered together and began the conference. They dined, they conferred, they disputed, they debated, they strolled, and they dined again. And when, after four changes of the moon and a day, they had sufficiently dined, conferred, disputed, debated, strolled, and dined again, they issued a communique in which they announced that in the spirit of unanimity and friendly cooperation, they had dined, conferred, disputed, debated, strolled, and dined again, and had finally come to this conclusion: they protested!

We protest against the unilateral violation of international customs which must be seen to have occurred in the procedures of the empire of Fox, where, with complete disregard for all the achievements of modern civilization, Fox has simply resorted to action. The powers represented at the conference, therefore, are unanimously resolved not to follow the fox empire on this path of violating the written and unwritten laws of international cooperation. The powers express their unanimous disapproval of the unilateral action taken by the fox empire, and they see themselves forced to declare that for their part they must refuse to answer the unilateral action of the fox empire with an act of their own. The powers rather feel that the fox empire must bear the onus of the one-sided consequences of its actions which are contrary to existing compacts.

When the Great Fox was confronted with the resolution of the conference of crows, he smiled and, being in a good mood, summoned his minister of education, and said to him, "I want the students of my land to be given the following test question, 'What is worth more—one power or a conference of powers?' Whichever of my pupils answers the question correctly, him I can use. The others had better go back and study some more."

Then he brushed the whiskers of his snout, sat down before his throne of maps, and ordered, "Send me the generals! I have worked up an appetite!"

18.

## The Foolish Cousins

It happened that the world was one day thrown into great excitement. Travelers and newspapers reported that the entire prairie was in flames. More and more inhabitants were fleeing the land where the fire raged, and ever more threateningly the cry "The jackals are loose!" rang through the world. "Howling and plundering they sweep through the world!

They have united with the predatory animals and they rule with bloody snouts! Save us from the jackals!"

Then the Great Fox appeared before the world and announced (and the parrots parroted him), "Have we not always said that the jackals threaten the world? Look to us! In our land there are no jackals! In our land no prairies are in flames! With our bodies we have established a bulwark against the red flood of jackals which is threatening to devour you. Just listen to the howling of the insatiable rabble at your borders! Now you see, do you not, that there is only one who protects you from the predatory instincts of the unloosed jackals? Only one—the Great Fox!"

"Yes, the Great Fox!" It echoed through the land.

With victorious mien, the Great One turned to his followers. One of them stood there before him and asked, "Great Fox, have you not yourself once announced that the blood which flows through the jackals' veins is the very foxes' blood which flows in us? What if the world should remember that we too have bloody snouts?"

"The world will not remember!" replied Fox. "I have always relied on the world's forgetfulness! Nothing is more certain than that. So let the jackals burn and devour and plunder. This is good for us! We foxes will appear all the more virtuous, the worse the others behave. As for the fact that they have the same blood and the same instincts as we do . . . who remembers that? The jackals are stupid, and that is what separates them from us. We are predators, but they do the howling and the frightened world comes running to us who appear peaceful.

"We do not tell the world that we are predators. And so, you see, the world has forgotten it."

### 19.

### High Treason

At this time the Great Fox gathered together his loyal followers and said, "Lately I have noticed some rather weird saints in my kingdom. A short while ago, as I was stalking through the grass for a little recreation, I came upon a horrible old spidery thing. He lay in the grass revealing his bigotry by raising his hands toward heaven instead of doing something sensible for the common good. And in this manner he was snagging the nicest insects out of the air."

"That was the praying mantis," explained one of Fox's counselors.

"Ah, so it was," Fox acknowledged, and then continued. "And then, in the forest, I saw some creeping creatures which had retreated into cells in the barks of trees. I couldn't see that they were doing anything worth-while—only eating!"

"Surely," a young fox hastened to explain, "those were the destructive caterpillars who later on become nun-moths and go about sucking all the sweetness out of everything they touch. Supplied with such virgin honey they sail through the land in their black and white costumes."

"Mmm. So they do," replied the Great Fox and then continued. "Then explain this. Yesterday a bird with a black spot on his head dared to enter my private garden. He sang, but he did not sing the victorious songs of our fox revolution! He kept right on singing, and although he must have noticed me, he did not once sing 'Zeeg!'"

"If he had a black spot on his head, he must have been the monkbird," one of the foxes assured him.

"Oh?" said Fox, and then continued. "What about all these creatures?

What do they do? Monkbirds and nun-moths! Have we any organizations for them? Then maybe that too was a monk, some fellow wearing a hood, brown as we are, whom I saw the other day walking through the fields endlessly preaching 'Praise the Lord!' He even dared to address me! 'May God be with you, brother fox!' he said!"

"Yes, that too was a monk," all the other foxes acknowledged.

And one explained, "They even preach to the fishes!"

And a second fox added, "That is their daily work."

And a third one, "They have nothing else to do."

And a fourth, "They teach all the creatures that they must praise some god other than you."

And a fifth one explained, "Yes, that is the way they seduce creatures."

And yet a sixth fox added, "There are entire organizations which do nothing else but that, such as the larks, the blackbirds, the nightingales, and the quails. Indeed, the quails are endlessly crying 'Feeeaargaaawd, feeeaargaaawd!' And they all withold their broods from us!"

At that the Great Fox became furious and he screamed, "They cry WHAT? Did you say 'Fear God! Fear God!'? I'll teach them to fear!"

One of Fox's advisors, who was seated on a large basket, remarked rather shrewdly, "You know, Great Fox, it is only some of the old ones who do this sort of thing any more. The young ones we have long since taught to worship you."

"Exterminate them!" yelled the Great Fox. "They are traitorous rabble! What they do is treason! High treason, I tell you! They tear down the community of foxes which we have finally achieved! They destroy the unanimity of the will of the foxes! They are the gravediggers of our unity! I have tolerated them long enough! I have *spared* them long enough! I did not break the shells of their eggs, but now my patience has come to an end! Go out in every direction and teach them, it is I who creates the eternal empire of foxes! He who opposes me is our enemy! Stamp out whoever is our enemy! Fear Fox! That is the commandment! And that shall be the prayer of my empire! No other prayer shall be said by my subjects than this one 'Fear Fox!' Now out with all of you! Teach them to fear me if they haven't learned to love me!"

At this command, the foxes raced off to the chicken coops, the pigeon lofts, and the songbirds' nests throughout the land, doing the will of Fox. And the black dogs were let loose to fall upon the hares: the tame ones, the wild ones, the black ones, the white ones, the brown ones, and the black-and-white ones. And they made a clean sweep of those whom they had up to now spared, those who still sang the praises they had been taught of old.

Beyond the mountains, however, the cardinal fidgeted about when he heard the news. He fluttered excitedly back and forth between the shimmering, butterfly-winged cardinals and the vari-splendored underwing moths. He was in such a state because in the empire of the Great Fox he had been accused and was about to be tried *in absentia*. Very nervously he kept shouting, "You have made the Great Fox angry. You must be quiet, very quiet, so he can be appeased."

20.

## Fox Visits His Relatives

In the meantime the boundaries of Fox's empire were extending farther and farther. The Great Fox who, as it was known from the lesser foxes and especially the parrots, had subsisted ascetically on nothing but roots and herbs during the early years of his power had now increased in might, and his lust for power left him with an ever-present appetite. With his subjects, whom he had well prepared for such excursions, he was now off to visit his relatives, first off some cousins in the east with whom he celebrated a joyous blood reunion. They had a grand time. Next he sought out his relatives whom he had fled in his youth because they had so misunderstood him. He joined with several of his staunch blood brothers in a great, conciliatory feast, and the rest of his relations sat around the table with tears of emotion in their eyes. Then the Great Fox stood up to propose a toast.

"Once upon a time we did not understand each other," he declared, "but now we have united!" And as a symbol of this union, he crammed a bloody morsel between his teeth.

"How generous he is," confessed the survivors, "he could have devoured us too and he didn't do it."

Now more and more relatives wanted to see Fox, and more and more asked for his visit. And thus what the parrots had been saying all along became obvious: that those with fox blood in their veins had everywhere lived oppressed and enslaved, and only now, since the Great Fox had come to redeem them, were they beginning really to live. And he redeemed more and more of his species, even deigning to liberate creatures who were not direct descendants of his race. For wherever a voice called for him there was revealed to Fox the further proof that some hidden bloodline of the fox race must have been awakened to consciousness. For only the inherited racial strain of the fox would have been able to produce the desire for fox liberation. And Fox incorporated them all because he was good.

In this manner, the Great Fox traveled to the north, the northeast, the south, the southeast, the west, and the northwest, and wherever he went he met new relatives.

At this same time the crows assembled again as representatives of their states. For moral reasons they had given up describing themselves with the brutal tag of "powers." Indeed, the crows now gathered even more frequently than before, and in their daily schedule there was soon only one item of business on the agenda: the taking of the roll. Whenever they met they congratulated each other that they were still uneaten and, so that no one's spiritual equilibrium would be threatened, they lost no words over those who had been devoured. It came to pass, however, that one day they felt moved to send a cordially phrased telegram of thanks to the Great Fox expressing the gratitude he deserved for reducing their budget. Previously they had had to meet in a palace and later in a great hall simply to accommodate the large number of delegates, whereas they now needed only a hotel room for their meetings. They continued, however, to issue communiques from their conferences, in which one could read that in the spirit of unanimity and cooperation, they had dined, conferred, disputed, debated, strolled, and dined again—only protesting had gone out of season. For that would merely have complicated the good relations with the great power of Fox, and it would have been immoral to burden the peace of the world with such a matter as the surrender of personal comforts.

55

**21.**

## As Wolf Encountered Fox

One warm, late-summer evening the Great Fox went for a stroll. All alone he wandered through the woods and the underbrush at the forest's edge, tending more and more eastward so that the sun, setting in the western sky, would not blind him.

"Soon the sign of the rising sun will again appear above you," he thought to himself as he watched the reflection of the western sunset in the fading light of the east. He was content with himself. Whenever he encountered any creatures, deer or squirrels, rabbits or stags, elk or birds, they all yielded to him respectfully or they hid themselves humbly from his eyes. "Yes, I am respected in my empire," he mused, "and soon my empire will be the world! How great I have become," he meditated, "since I began to realize that the secret of success is nothing but simple insolence."

While he had thus been ambling through the grass, dusk had fallen. The Great Fox continued on farther and farther eastward toward his soon-rising sun. Now he came upon a vast, unbounded plain and soon he saw nothing in front of him except that through the blurry sea of gray which reflected the last remnants of daylight, he could make out two lights, still far away but close together. Fox scurried soundlessly through the already dew-dampened grass of the steppe, heading in the direction of the lights.

Now he saw them, then he didn't, now they seemed nearer, then extinguished.

Suddenly from in front of him a warm wind—no, a hot breath—blew directly into his face! Before him gleamed the greedy, narrowed eyes of a wolf. Fox's mortal enemy!

"Oh! Comrade Wolf!" Fox quickly composed himself.

"Comrade?" the other one asked.

"Why we are indeed relatives, aren't we?" Fox hastened to add. "We belong to the same canine family! Surely you know to what honors I have elevated our race?"

"And yet you have been only a thief," panted Wolf contemptuously. The fox did not feel at all comfortable since, after an impressive pause, Wolf repeated, "Have been . . . !"

But the fox tried to rally with a jest. "Well, you . . . ah . . . aren't exactly a very polite cousin, are you?"

Wolf's red tongue rolled out of his mouth and he snarled, "You have, of course, stolen my ideas, but all the while you were only laying the groundwork for me!"

"Laying the groundwork! Listen to him!" the fox began in an effort to impress his opponent.

But Wolf blew his hot breath into the other's face so vigorously that the fox had to shut his eyes. And in that instant, Wolf jumped him. Soundlessly he pinned him to the ground. Then Wolf sank his fangs into the Great Fox's neck!

∎

The rising sun illuminated a naked, battle-trampled, stone plateau from which all greenery had been stripped and strewn about in every direction by the biting morning wind, never to be found again. Earlier there must have been many wolves there under the moonlight for not even a trace of the Fox's remains could anywhere be seen. Where before millions of living things had bustled about in the mossy thickness, the sun now burned even the last damp patches dry until nothing remained but denuded stone. Only one crumb of earth had clung fast to where a rock slab fell on an incline to one side offering protection from the wind. And if one had looked closely he might have seen a few tiny shreds of living lichen staunchly and stubbornly embracing the tiny clod. They did not release their grip only because their beginning seemed so hopeless and so empty. They knew that the new life of the future depended upon their tenuous, wretched hold, and on a fidelity and obedience to the will of a providence which had placed them here in the boundless isolation of this plateau, not as the accidental victims of a whim, but in that wisdom which broods in eternities. And they also knew that it would take many years perhaps until a green family might once again gather around them, and perhaps decades until the first barren stone would be spun about by the fecundity of healthy, swelling tufts of moss, and that all this, as well as the new, century-long growth, could not come to pass out of this coming fruitfulness if they would now release their hold only to be strewn about by the wind.

For even in nature the Creator has chosen for the beginning of all great things the small and the unlikely.

# Notes

1.

Fox and the Foxes

*". . . he ran away to his relatives."*
Hitler's leaving Austria for Germany.

*"My brothers! We are of the same kind, of the same color."*

The fox's speech, as well as the majority of the speeches in the *Fuchsenfabeln*, is tailored closely to the style and demagogic argumentation of typical Nazi Party speeches. The following example of Hitler oratory (Reichstag speech of March 23, 1933) demonstrates the kind of Nazi ideology, and the language in which it was expressed, which Knab parodied throughout the *Fuchsenfabeln*.

> Simultaneously with this political purification of our public life, the Government of the Reich will undertake a thorough moral purging of the body corporate of the nation. *The entire educational system, the theater, the cinema, literature, the Press, and the wireless—all these will be used as means to this end and valued accordingly.* They must all serve for the maintenance of the eternal values present in the essential character of our people. Art will always remain the expression and the reflection of the longings and the realities of an era. The neutral international attitude of aloofness is rapidly disappearing. Heroism is coming forward passionately and will in the future shape and lead political destiny. It is the task of art to be the expression of this determining spirit of the age. Blood and race will once more become the source of artistic intuition.[1]

2.
The Ostrich, Fox, and, Then Again, the Ostrich

*". . . Sir Ostrich was attending a footrace . . . ."*

The ostrich represents Franz von Papen specifically, and the somewhat decadent aristocracy in general. Von Papen's physical endowments, his somewhat scrawny face and long neck, are appropriately represented in the ostrich. The opening line is a general reference to the aristocrat's penchant for horseracing.

*". . . several occasions of disrespect among the chickens . . . ."*

In 1933, in Munich, von Papen, main speaker at an international *Katholik Gesellentag,* was shouted down by his audience.

*". . . the Great One sent the ostrich packing."*

Hitler's appointment of von Papen as ambassador to Austria after the Blood Purge of June 30, 1934, when von Papen's usefulness as a Hitler cabinet member had ended.

---

[1] Adolf Hitler, *My New Order,* pp.152-3.

3.

Stewings and Doings among the Feathered-Folk

The "feathered-folk" represent the traditional leadership classes in pre-Nazi society: the educational, professional, and ecclesiastical leaders. Concerning this fable, Knab says:

> These leaders and the organizations they represented (for example the para-military Stahlhelm, an organization of Hugenberg's Deutschnationale Partei) supposedly represented the steadying influence of traditional law and order. The surrender and dissolution of these organizations was one of the most fatal occurrences in the then German society. It not only withdrew in the eyes of many the aura of respectability from all anti-Nazi opposition; it made surrender to the Nazi regime almost a point of national honor.[2]

*". . . one of Fox's burrows collapsed."*
Reference to the Blood Purge of June 30, 1934.

4.

The Cardinal and the Birdlover

The cardinal represents Monsignor Kaas, leader of the predominantly Catholic Center Party. I have translated as "cardinal" the German word *Dompfaff* which means "bullfinch"; *Pfaff* means "cleric," "priest," or "parson." To retain the clerical connotations of the German I have used the word "cardinal." (The cardinal is a member of the finch family.)

*". . . hung some cages . . . ."*

Knab makes the following comment on this fable:

> The bird cages with the roughed-up birds refer to the Catholic members of the Reichstag, Landtag, and Catholic editors and other organizational leaders in Nazi "protective custody," the preferred euphemism for concentration camps at the time. In this scene the "cardinal" is negotiating the surrender of the Church's secular organizations in return for his and his party's cooperation with the Nazi regime. He is thus preparing the way for the Concordat between the Vatican and the Nazi state in which the paper existence of the Catholic organizations was "guaranteed."[3]

*". . . flew off across the mountains."*

Kaas's voluntary exile to Rome, where he was employed as a Vatican archeologist.

5.

The Feeding

In this and the remaining fables I have chosen to retain the sound of the German *Sieg* with the made-up word "zeeg."

*". . . first 'Zeeg!' then feed: first bow. then chow."*

This is a free translation of *"Erst: Sieg. dann Brocken! Erst Dank, dann*

---

[2] Knab, *Interview.*
[3] Knab, *Interview.*

*Frass."* Here, and throughout the fables, I have taken liberties in order to provide an idiomatically acceptable translation. *The Feeding* satirizes the Nazi Winterhilfe, or winter relief program; first proof of loyalty, then relief.

### 6.

### The Weasel

The German *Marder* is a pine marten, a member of the weasel family, though somewhat larger than the weasel. Both animals indulge in the habit of sucking eggs without breaking the shells. I have translated *Marder* as "weasel," because the latter is more commonly known in this country, and the connotations of sneakiness and treachery are, for us, more readily evoked by the weasel than the marten.

Specifically, the weasel represents Hanns Kerrl, Minister of Ecclesiastical Affairs. The fable generally satirizes Hitler's treatment of the Church and the Concordat between the Vatican and the Nazi state, which was formally signed and sealed on July 20, 1933.

*". . . very irksome contract . . . . 'contractual eggs.' "*
References to the Concordat and its various conditions.

*"black nest"*
The Center Party and its southern offspring, the Bavarian People's Party.

### 7.

### How Fox Encountered the Various Animals

*"black dog"*
The S. S.

*"a rich hamster"*
The business community.

*"the tiniest insect"*
The fable uses the insect and the rest of the bugs and flies to satirize police methods.

*"the old lion"*
A reference to the remaining monarchical families (for example, Crown Prince Rupprecht of Bavaria) who were shown respect when it seemed politically expedient to Hitler.

8.

The Parrot Plague

*"Jako, the gray parrot"*

    Dr. Joseph Goebbels, Hitler's Propaganda Minister.

*"half-demented ones"*

    Those propagandists, shaken, though only momentarily, out of the stupor in which their own propaganda had placed them.

9.

How the Fishes Were Rewarded

*"the fishes"*

    The so-called unpolitical or nonpolitical people, and also the vast mass who were uneasy but "knew better" than to ask questions.

10.

Schoolmaster Fly and the Cuckoo Parents

*"ichneumon flies"*

    These insects are noted for their habit of laying their eggs on or beneath the skin of the larvae that they have selected for their young to prey upon. They are used in this fable to satirize what went on particularly in primary education under Hitler.

*"the cuckoos"*

    Cuckoos frequently lay their eggs into the nests of other birds.

11.

The Wise Owls

*"Bubu the eagle owl"*

    Bernhard Rust, Reich Minister of Science, Education and Popular Culture.

*". . . so that the world may recover its health."*

    An ironic reference to the philosopher Johann Gottlieb Fichte's saying *"Am deutschen Wesen muss die Welt genesen."*

12.

The Envy of the Woodpeckers

*"the black woodpeckers"*

    A reference to Catholic jurists.

*"The conifer underworld"*

    Common criminals.

*". . . and one black woodpecker, a professor of law . . . ."*

Dr. Carl Schmitt, Catholic professor at the University of Berlin. After 1933, he made a complete about-face and became, among other things, leader of the University Teachers in the Federation of National Socialist Preservers of Law. What the black woodpecker loudly exclaims about the fox's will being the supreme law is, according to Knab, an almost direct quotation of a statement Schmitt made before an audience of jurists soon after the June 30, 1934, Purge.

13.

"Fuchs, Du hast . . ."

The title of this fable is made up of the first three words of a German children's song. Since at the end of the first paragraph, an entire line of the song is cited, I chose to include a parenthetical translation there and to retain the German title in an effort to capture the feeling of the original.

*" . . . six days after the summer solstice . . . ."*

June 30, 1934, the date of Hitler's Blood Purge.

*" . . . grouse who were romping amorously in the grass . . ."*

A satiric reference to alleged homosexual practices among many members of the S.A. Otto Dietrich, Hitler's press chief at the time of the Purge, made much of the depraved morals of the S.A. leaders, and claimed that Lieutenant Edmund Heines, shot in the Purge, was found in bed with a young man.[4]

*" . . . even a few parrots had been slaughtered."*

In the Purge, a few loyal Nazis were shot by mistake.

*"the butcherbird"*

The butcherbird represents Heinrich Himmler, who was made head of the Prussian Gestapo on April 1, 1934, and Chief of the Federal Police by statute of June 17, 1936. The butcherbird is a shrike, known for its peculiar habit of impaling its victims on the thorns of its nest.

14.

The Much-Traveled Bison

About this fable, Knab says: "The fable uses a true story about Hermann Göring, who received a prize Russian bull for his hunting preserve from the Russian Government. The story was included to illustrate the basic parallelism between one totalitarian regime and another."[5]

---

[4] William L. Shirer, *The Rise and Fall of the Third Reich* (Greenwich: Fawcett Publications, Inc., A Crest Reprint, 1965), p. 312.

[5] Knab, *Interview.*

15.

## The Migratory Birds Begin Their Travels

*". . . gain strength through joy."*

A direct reference to Kraft durch Freude, an organization directed by Dr. Robert Ley, which provided regimented leisure for the people of Hitler's Reich.

*". . . their wings were clipped . . ."*

The confiscation of passports, which prevented anyone suspected by the regime from leaving the country.

*"wealthy cranes . . . aristocratic herons"*

The well-heeled tourists and playboys who came to Germany, but remarked none of the seamier occurrences. They left the country again, praising the Third Reich because the trains ran on time.

16.

## Reporter Stork Goes Interviewing

The stork represents no one person in particular, but the irony is directed to the gullibility of international journalism.

*". . . errors in counting . . . ."*

About Jako's (Goebbels') answers, Knab says: "What Jako says about Nazi elections is based upon actual Goebbels' directives; namely to count all anti-Hitler votes as pro votes, because only old age, imbecility or momentary confusion could have led a German to vote against the Führer."[6]

17.

## The Conference of the Crows

*". . . they were considered to be the most peaceful of all animals . . . ."*

The crows' general structure and intelligence have caused them to be regarded as the highest type of bird.

*"We protest against the unilateral violation . . ."*

I have taken the liberty of separating the crows' statement of protest from the narrative in order to give it more of the flavor of a committee statement. The German text is expressed in the third person: *"Sie protestierten gegen . . . ,"* whereas I have translated the passage: "We protest against . . ." Here I was after effect; but the change does not alter the meaning.

---

[6] Knab, *Interview*.

18.

The Foolish Cousins

*". . . entire prairie was in flames."*

Reference to the Spanish Civil War, which broke out in the summer of 1936.

19.

High Treason

*"monkbird . . . nun-moth"*

It is likely that the German *Mönchsgrasmücke* and *Nonnen* are names that go back to medieval times. What is important for the purposes of the translation is that the English language has a monkbird and a nun-moth. Even if they are not the exact zoological equivalents of the German creatures, their use in this fable adequately and appropriately conveys their role as representatives of various religious orders.

*"underwing moths"*

The underwing moth (*Ordensbandfalter*) has brightly colored underwings.

*"Very nervously he kept shouting . . . ."*

Monsignor Kaas continued to give out advice from his hideaway in Rome.

20.

Fox Visits His Relatives

Knab wrote this fable between two and three years before Hitler absorbed Austria, Poland, Yugoslavia, Latvia, etc.

*". . . he sought out his relatives whom he had fled in his youth . . ."*

A reference to the incorporation of Austria into the Third Reich.

*". . . more and more asked for his visit."*

A reference to men such as Quisling in Norway, who helped soften up their countries for the eventual Nazi occupation.

21.

As Wolf Encountered Fox

Knab recalls that in the summer of 1936 news of the increasing military build-up in Germany gave one who daily observed these developments a sense of impending doom. He, and many friends with whom he discussed the news from Germany, gradually came more and more to feel that civilization might well be destroyed when the armies would inevitably clash. It is such a conviction that sets the tone for this last, prophetic fable.

Regarding this fable, Knab says:

This last fable can, of course, claim only partial correctness in the realm of historical reality. The two totalitarianisms did clash, and the clash ended with the disappearance of the one which, beyond the naked use of power for the sake of national egoism, had no deep or unifying idea of universal appeal; it offered only slavery for all those who would fall under it. Nazi totalitarianism denied the humanity of human actions to its own adherents; it enslaved the masters in their own inhumanity. In Nazism, the only end to look forward to was hell; it had to break on its own inhumanity.

In communism are resurrected, in purely secularized forms, the same universal ideals which could have transformed Western society, had historical Christianity not betrayed—or should I say abandoned—these ideals. They survived in the heroic lives of individuals only, but could not find universal acceptance. So the Christian ideals have come down to us in perverted form, though still containing the power of the universal longing for justice which makes people willing to sacrifice for a paradise to come.

The "epilogue" was written out of a conviction that the last "great" war could have ended with the desolation depicted there. The next one will. In the face of the precariousness of history, I have nothing to offer but the hope—of my Christian faith.[7]

---

[7] Knab, *Interview.*

# APPENDIX 1

## Knab's "An Editorial That Can No Longer Be Printed"

The following is my translation of Otto Michael Knab's "Ein Leitartikel, der nicht mehr gedruckt werden darf,'" which was published for the first time on July 22, 1965, in the ninetieth anniversary issue of the Starnberg *Land und Seebote.*  The article, written on July 14, 1934, the night before Knab escaped from his native Germany into Switzerland, evidences its author's struggle with his own conscience as editor of a daily newspaper within the Nazi state.

Just as a man might react to a rival party's successful acquisition of power by hoping in good faith that it will tone down some of its radical campaign pronouncements and begin working in the best interests of the country, so Knab first responded to the Nazi Party's ascension to power in January, 1933.  But his cautious optimism was soon tried far beyond what he in conscience could abide.

"Never would I have believed that it would be in this manner that I must take leave of our readers with whom, as editor of the *Land und Seebote,* I have felt the closest ties for these last ten years.  I must do it, because I do not want the abuse the Nazis will pour out against me to go unanswered, and I therefore ask all who receive this editorial to pass it on.

"When, in 1933, under pressure the extent of which cannot yet be revealed, the *Land und Seebote* was converted into an organ of the Nazi state, I resolved after great inner conflicts (those who know me know about them) to remain as editor if I were permitted to do so.  I did not make this decision for the sake of my family, but in order to prevent an extreme radical from turning our hometown paper into a hatesheet.  And I did so also in the hope of preventing at least some of the worst excesses, and of mitigating the inevitable.  This was my first reason.

"In the course of the months when Hitler's government seemed step by step to show signs of recovery, I approached the new ideas with more and more good will, prompted also by a certain sense of obligatory decency because of the fact that Kreisleiter Buchner had not removed me from my job as he could have done. And when I reached the point in my own mind where I believed I could justify it to myself, I wrote the first articles in support of the new state. Not a day sooner!

"Mine was not a change of view from one day to another, no mere outward getting in line. Only when I had come a few steps closer during this last winter to trusting my own good will, did I undertake in about seventy articles to ask honestly for the cooperation and good will of those who still stood aside. Always, I was guided by the motivation: what is at stake is not the fate of the NSDAP, but the fate of Germany.

"Then began, in the spring, the unequivocal attack on Christianity, not openly, not led by the Führer himself, but initiated by Rosenberg on the Führer's orders, and received with enthusiasm by all the subordinate Führers in the land. The same spirit again came into bloom which made Gauleiter Adolf Wagner stifle in blood the Young Catholic Workers congress in 1933. Go to Ellwangen in Thuringia—you will hear what happened there this year. The Nazi leadership school there trampled on the crucifix in the public square. The symbol of the cross was banned. But one cannot root it out in this way, just as Christ cannot be rooted out.

"But enough! It is not possible to enumerate all the details here. Now also, in Starnberg, began the pressure against our paper. I have never denied my Catholic views, and during all this time I have specifically emphasized them in my editorials, articles which were not narrowly denominational, but simply and fundamentally Christian. But this, of course, got on the gentlemen's nerves. Naturally it would—when the Kreisleiter himself dared say in a speech last year to medical doctors, and this year in an address to teachers, that Christianity had lasted for two thousand years, but is now all over; in the place of Christ there now stands Adolf Hitler. Naturally it would—when the same Kreisleiter writes in his daughter's diary: 'You need not love your neighbors, but your enemies you must hate,' and then commences to preach national fellowship (*Gemeinschaft*) to the people for propaganda purposes. But publicly, of course, the personal views of our Kreisleiter are carefully masked. That is why he let me stay on for a while, why he seemed to take my side in x-number of conversations—until eight days ago that is.

"Within two hours, our powerful Kreisleiter Mr. Buchner managed to turn the opinions and instructions he had previously expressed to me into the exact opposite. In a conference among Buchner, Einhauser, and myself, and in the presence of Kreysern and Vonwerden, Buchner confronted me with conditions which are first of all against the law, and which secondly make it impossible for me in conscience to work further for the new state. Buchner today threw in my face the very Christian articles with which before he had pretended to agree. He dictated that I would no longer have the right, as the press law prescribes it, to edit the paper in accordance with my own judgment, but that without any say whatsoever I would have to print what the gentlemen mentioned would choose to serve up to me. I am being forced, as the article 'The Duties of a Newspaper' on Thursday of this week proves, to print things which constitute incitement against German citizens, and which make us spit upon ourselves. I would need only to take the responsibility for everything, and underwrite it all with my name. This 'conference' ended with a threat.

"I have drawn the following conclusions from what has occurred.

"1. My work has lost all defensible meaning before my conscience.

"2. It is in conscience and in character impossible for me to work under this suppression.

"3. The hope for justice no longer exists in our 'constitutional state.' (In answer to my request that proceedings be initiated against me within the provisions of the press law, Buchner replied, 'That we will not do. You would certainly win such a process. We want something quite different.')

"4. To save my conscience, I must now, like so many thousands upon thousands in our country, change from a man of good will into one who rejects this system, which in its lack of civilized values is distinguished from Bolshevism at most in degree, but not in kind.

"I cannot do otherwise. My conscience demands it. Upright men are no longer tolerated in Germany. They are put against the wall, or thrown into concentration camps. So the only avenue left to me is emigration. I shall take a handful of German soil with me, and upon it I pledge: I will be a worker for a free Germany.

"Willingly do I leave behind for this goal everything I have built up for myself. I leave with a last thanks to all with whom and for whom I have been privileged to work, and I greet them all in the hope of a coming free land of justice, of honor, and of the Christian spirit.

"Everything for Germany! Germany for Christ!

"And now they may spit on me!"

# APPENDIX 2

## Knab's Earlier Fables

The following is my translation of two fables that were written by Otto Knab nearly two years before he began writing the *Fuchsenfabeln*. Both of these fables appeared in the *Land und Seebote* during the month of January, 1934. By this time, the *Land und Seebote* had been taken over by the Nazis, and the swastika appeared on the masthead of the paper. The second fable has no title, but simply begins after Knab has written that the swineherd story in the play he has reviewed has prompted him to tell another little story.

# I

*"Peep"*

" 'Peep!' A bird pecks at the window. The habitual feeding place is empty today, out of forgetfulness. He is hungry. Several are hungry. Many are hungry. Many are freezing. In such circumstances there is nothing better than some solid food in the stomach to warm one. But there is no food. The bacon rind is missing. The kernels are missing. What's going on? 'Peep, peep!' It already sounds a little more energetic. After all, one has a right to it. Perhaps the feathered ones have heard something about the prescriptive law? They certainly need it. We believe they need it. Some of them are very well nourished as far as is visible on the outside. They are the ones peeping the loudest. But the others, the quiet ones in the background, they have such begging, longing eyes, that we cannot hesitate any longer. Open the window. Swish! They are all gone. But as soon as the rind of bacon and the handfuls of kernels are delivered, the birds all come back again and gratefully let us watch them enjoy their contentment. Let us not be less concerned about the starving and freezing among our own people than we are for the birds in winter. Once again, it is 'One-pot Sunday.' There is room for all around the common table of the nation. No one should shame himself by failing to contribute to the common good."

About *"Peep,"* Knab says the following:

"One-pot Sunday" had been introduced by the Nazi state.  The idea was that once a month the people should partake of only a simple one-pot meal and turn the money thus saved over to the Nazi winter relief program.  In practice, all that was required was a substantial contribution.[1]

# II

"Once upon a time there was a woodpecker.  He lived in a little forest by the lake and did as the other woodpeckers in larger forests do.  He kept his trees clean of insects and larvae, and as was unavoidable, wherever he hammered, there was some splintering.  The forest, however, was so small that he was the only woodpecker in it.  And because he was by origin a black woodpecker, there were many birds who disliked him.  They reasoned, 'Why does the woodpecker have to hammer?  We certainly don't hammer!'

"Now in this little forest, there also stood a very healthy young tree. The woodpecker did not have to hammer on it, because the tree was free of insects.  But one time the woodpecker's eye had discovered some insects even on this healthy tree, and as soon as he had discovered them he climbed up and started tap-tapping.  He needed only to tap, not hammer, because nothing was rotten.  He snagged himself a few insects, ate them, and then left the scene.  But now the other birds became very indignant, and they wanted to drag the woodpecker before a court of non-woodpeckers.  Some even went so far as to fly to the master of the forest and ask him to shoot the woodpecker.  It was unheard of, they said, that the woodpecker should busy himself tapping on such a healthy tree.  At the very least, he should be forbidden to hammer at it.  But the forester was a wise man, who knew well that some of his birds must sing, and others must hammer.  So he did not shoot the only woodpecker in his forest, nor did he replace him with a senile or blind one.  He knew that the tapping of the woodpecker was not to be excluded in the concert of the forest.  And he knew his woodpecker as one who never looked at the trees on which he hammered, but who spotted only the crevasses where the insects burrowed.  And he said to himself, 'The woodpecker has already made much in the little forest clean.  He ought to go on looking for insects and cleaning them out wherever he finds them.'

"And so the woodpecker keeps right on tapping.  And when it must be, he hammers as well."

Knab has commented briefly on this fable:

The woodpecker is the editor (myself) of the *Land und Seebote*. Quite a few of

---

[1] Knab, *Interview*.

our readers were aware that at that time I was under surveillance and attack by some of the local Nazis who were (with reason, I admit) dissatisfied with my editorial direction of the newspaper, which in fact they had a right to control. Up to that time I had the local Nazi chief on my side—or so it seemed. This fable was an attempt to strengthen both my own position and what I assumed to be his. The healthy tree was to symbolize what the Nazi Party claimed to be. The insects are a reference to incidents of local corruption to which some of my writings had indirectly alluded. The forester was the local Nazi chief (Buchner). My attempt to save a doomed situation failed, of course. The fable was written in January, 1934. In July of that year I escaped from Germany into Switzerland.[2]

---

[2] Knab, *Interview*.